SOLVING GLOBAL WARMING WILL KILL THE FOSSIL FUEL INDUSTRY

Thomas Miezejeski

 Published by Brookside Press, 211 D Manchester Dr., Basking Ridge NJ 07920

Please leave a review

Reviews of the fuel of the publishing industry. Even a review of a few sentences would be greatly appreciated. Reviewers are the primary way that readers determine if they're going to purchase a book, especially self-published books. We also ask that you share your takeaways from this book with your friends, family and associates. If you find this book interesting, it should be interesting to your associates as well.

Table of Contents

Introduction

Storm Warning

This book is a storm warning. As with a natural event like a hurricane or a blizzard there's not much we can do about changing the course that the storm will take. But by warning the people in the path of the storm it's possible to mitigate the damage that will occur and the loss of life if the warning did not exist. Global warming is presenting an existential threat to society as we know it today. There are some steps that can be taken to impact the effect of global warming, and these steps have already started to be taken. However, there will be many consequences which are not fully anticipated at this time. Those people that take note now will avoid some negative consequences.

This book is also an attempt to understand the true problem we face. The first step in solving a problem is to understand what the problem is, what its causes are, and outline possible alternative solutions. Then the most effective action can be taken to solve the problem at hand.

The purpose of this book is not to convince people that global warming is in fact occurring and will have consequences beyond our control if we don't do anything now to solve it. If you are convinced that global warming is not a problem, read no more.

Global warming is a problem where people have tended to take sides rather than unifying with a common effort to solve the problem. The fossil fuel industry, one of the largest segments of the world economy, was the 1st to recognize the potential consequences of burning fossil fuels and increasing CO2 and methane in the atmosphere.

If you are an executive in the fossil fuel industry It's easy to declare that the industry has done a very good job in protecting its assets and maintaining its profits. Its efforts have extended the life of the industry by at least 20 years and maybe even 40 years. Unfortunately, the industry has been withdrawing from the environmental bank and society as a whole must now pay the consequences to solve the problem before it gets out of control.

In writing this book I have not tried to take sides in this problem. We would not enjoy the way of life that we have today if it was not for the fossil fuel industry. The industry allowed the world economy to move from a mostly agricultural society to a sophisticated and complex society with most people now engaged with goods and services other than agricultural products. However, we have arrived at that point where we can no longer ask future generations to pay for the benefits we are experiencing today.

Even the fossil fuel industry can benefit from the information in this book since it can help them mitigate negative consequences if it is no longer able to preserve the dominant position that it now maintains in the world economy.

There is an old expression "Be careful about what you wish for because you just might get it". What is implied in this statement is that all consequences of getting what your wish for may not be what you expected.

The existential issue of our time is global warming. After a period of controversy over whether global warming was really occurring and whether it was humanly caused, most people generally agree that it is being caused by an increase in carbon dioxide and methane in the atmosphere. The major cause of this increase in these gases is because of burning fossil fuels. Thus, the solution to the problem is to eliminate fossil fuels and replace them with other sources of energy such as renewable energy in the form of wind power, solar energy, hydroelectric, and nuclear energy from fission reactions, which fell out of favor, but is now receiving renewed interest as an additional source of energy.

Almost all the books today on global warming involve a description of the sources of carbon dioxide and methane and steps that can be taken to reduce or eliminate these emissions. Other books focus on the consequences of global warming such as more severe weather, rising sea levels because of glacial melting, and forest fires and droughts as a result of changing weather patterns.

Very little has been written about the impact of the demise of the fossil fuel industry which will be a consequence of solving global warming. While fusion technology has been on the distant horizon for many decades it now appears that this source of energy could be available within the next 20 years. If fusion technology is implemented, it will also result in the demise of the fossil fuel industry. Thus, this book is an examination of the potential impacts of the demise of the fossil fuel industry.

The fossil fuel energy industry generates annual revenues between $6 and $7 trillion annually. If the fossil fuel industry was a country it would be the third largest economy in the world ranking only behind the United States and China in gross domestic product. Another way of looking at this is to consider that the fossil fuel industry is greater than the entire output of Germany and Italy combined.

In July 2024 Ugewald and 17 NGO partners released the 2024 edition of investing in climate chaos. The website reveals that the fossil fuel industry holds over 7500 institutional investors worldwide. The data was retrieved in May 2024 and shows that institutional investors currently hold $4.3 trillion in bonds and shares of fossil fuel companies. These investments are held by pension funds, insurance companies, asset managers, hedge funds, sovereign wealth funds, endowment funds, and asset management arms of commercial banks.

Thus, the demise of the fossil fuel industry would not only result in the loss of significant revenues, but the decline in these companies could also present significant capital losses to current investors. This report also indicated that while the 2021 UN climate summit in Glasgow ended with an agreement to accelerate efforts towards phasing down of coal 52,160 institutional investors continue to hold bonds and shares in coal companies many of these investors claim to be engaged with the industry on global warming, but their engagements efforts have negligible impact. Over 95% of companies have failed to set a coal exit date and 40% are still planning to develop new coal assets investment in these companies are blocking the energy transition. The report also revealed that oil and gas companies are still exploring and developing new oil and gas reserves. The industry has increased its annual capital expenditure on oil and gas exploration by more than 30% since 2021

These activities are part of a corporate strategy for the fossil fuel companies often characterized as plausible denial. In other words, they denied that fossil fuels were causing global warming, although internal research indicated this to be the case many decades ago or recognized that global warming was occurring but took no actions to address it.

What I have learned from my experience

For a major part of my working career, I analyzed the impact and reported on technological change in several industry sectors such as telecommunications, computers, and financial services. Before that I was part of the long-range planning and investment analysis for several major Fortune 500 companies. An essential factor in all this work was an analysis of change, how it would happen and when it would happen. The major takes away from that experience has been that over the short term it's possible to analyze change and its impacts, but over the long term, which I would define as 10 years, the projections of change both in direction and intensity are usually way off the mark.

Two examples that can illustrate my point are changes that occurred at Smith Corona, which was the premier manufacturer of consumer typewriters in the United States in the 1970s and early 1980s and how AT&T was off the mark in its long-term planning for the telecommunications industry.

One of the major uses of personal computers when they were introduced was word processing. Personal computers allow individuals to write reports much more efficiently through the use of word processing programs and inkjet printers. Low-cost printers used in conjunction with affordable programs that allowed the creation of electronic documents made the typewriter obsolete in just a few short years. I don't know if any studies have been done but I imagine that the current generation of college students, who were the primary customers for consumer typewriters when I worked for Smith Corona, haven't even seen a typewriter in your entire lifetime.

In the early 1990s cell phones were becoming popular but were still expensive. AT&T assumed that they would be integrated with traditional wireline services. The company characterized this integration process as personal communication services where wireline phones in the home and the office and cell phones and pagers would all be coordinated by a centralized service. The intent of this service would be to allow the most efficient use of these services and make people more productive. As we all know as the cost of cell phones dropped the use of cell phones exploded as the market became more competitive and prices for phones and services dropped dramatically. Cell phone manufacturers also incorporated more functionality, so they became cameras and access devices for the Internet.

These two examples illustrate that even the best run companies do not anticipate the impact of technological change on their markets and their companies. In the case of Smith Corona, the technology change resulted in a workforce of thousands of people became obsolete and the equipment they used to manufacture their product also became unusable in the manufacture of printers. There was a significant difference between a laser printer and an electromechanical device such as the typewriter. This made it very difficult for people or the assets to transition to the new technology. Also, since the change resulted in a transition of an activity from one device to another there was not that much difference in the size of the market for the devices.

In the case of AT&T the cell phone industry was mostly incremental creating new revenues for the companies. The wireline resources we're still used for other services in the industry. In this case there were significant changes in which companies were the industry leaders and their approach to the marketplace in terms of advertising and promotion. The telecommunication industry transitioned from a regulated monopoly to a competitive market.

What's in this book

In this book I will describe how the demise of the fossil fuel industry will be more like the impact that computers had on typewriters than the transition experienced by the telecommunications industry as cell phones came to dominate the marketplace.

To understand this difference, it's important to understand some basics about energy and the differences between fossil fuels and renewable energy. Not only will there be significant incompatibilities between the infrastructure required for the fossil fuel industry and renewable energy eventual efficiencies will result in significant reductions in employment and assets employed in the industry.

Positive Impact of the fossil fuel industry

When people think about the fossil fuel industry, they could be considered villains because they are the cause of the emission of carbon dioxide and methane, which are the main causes of global warming. However, it's important to understand all the positive impacts that the fossil fuel industry has had on society over the last 200 years. These positive impacts have influenced both the companies and the consumers of their products to initially deny global warming and then resist the transition to other energy sources.

Worldwide impact of the demise of the Fossil Fuel Industry

With an industry as large as the fossil fuel industry it will not be possible to phase out this industry in a relatively short period of time without global impacts especially in States and economies, we're a significant portion of revenues are generated from fossil fuel exploration refining and distribution.

On a country-by-country basis we examine the various impacts on the top countries influenced by the demise of the fossil fuel industry

Cost of global warming over the next 25 years

In addition to the costs directly associated with the demise of this industry is important to look at the social economic environmental costs that will result i from global warming. Estimates of these costs range from 20 trillion to $40 trillion. The sooner we can transition from the fossil fuel industry to renewable energy the less the impact on global warming and the cost associated with mitigating and repairing the damages that will result.

Strategies to offset revenues losses due to global warming

The fossil fuel industry recognizes that it's its existence is it dressing the issue of the carbon dioxide and methane emitted as a result of the use of its products. These strategies include investing in renewable energy, carbon capture and storage and investments in technology that will reduce the emission of these gases while still continuing their use as an energy source.

Many people are skeptical about both the potential to solve the problem via these measures and the true commitment of the industry to implementing these changes. As would be expected the industry is planning for its continued existence rather than its demise which other people believe is the only alternative.

How will it happen

There is no question the demise of an industry of the proportions of the fossil fuel industry we'll have significant impacts. However the rate of the transition we'll also have a significant impact upon the ability to limit the negative impacts of this transition. We draw from experience from other major technology changes that have occurred in the past and projected them onto the fossil fuel industry. The primary purpose of this examination is to present an urgency to the problem which may not be present at this time.

Planning for the Demise

If one assumes that the demise of the fossil fuel industry is inevitable the best we can do is to plan for the most equitable demise which allows the industry to participate in its own demise and minimize the impact on the rest of society as a result of the demise.

Overview of the global warming problem.

While it is not the objective of this book to duplicate the information provided in other books with regard to the causes and progression of global warming it is important to have a quick review of the issue at hand to enable a common perspective in the analysis to follow.

The Paris Agreement, signed in 2015, set a critical target to limit the rise in global average temperature to well below 2°C above pre-industrial levels, with efforts to cap it at 1.5°C. However, current projections based on existing policies indicate a significant risk of exceeding the 2°C threshold within the coming decades.

2. Key Environmental Impacts

2.1 Increased Frequency and Severity of Extreme Weather Events

A rise in global temperatures intensifies the hydrological cycle, resulting in more extreme and frequent weather events:

- **Heatwaves**: More frequent and severe heatwaves will affect ecosystems, agriculture, and human health. Some regions could experience extreme, life-threatening heat conditions.
- **Storms and Hurricanes**: Warmer ocean waters will fuel more intense storms and hurricanes, resulting in greater damage to infrastructure, ecosystems, and coastal communities.
- **Flooding and Droughts**: Shifts in precipitation patterns will lead to both increased flood risks in some areas and longer, more severe droughts in others. This will challenge water availability, food production, and wildlife survival.

2.2 Sea-Level Rise

Exceeding 2°C of warming accelerates the melting of ice sheets in Greenland and Antarctica, as well as glaciers worldwide. As a result:

- **Coastal Erosion and Flooding**: Rising sea levels will cause greater coastal erosion, displace millions of people, and threaten habitats such as wetlands, estuaries, and coral reefs.

- **Loss of Small Island Nations**: Some low-lying island nations and coastal areas are at risk of becoming uninhabitable due to persistent flooding and erosion.

2.3 Disruption of Ecosystems and Loss of Biodiversity

A global temperature increase of more than 2°C will severely impact ecosystems and species:

- **Habitat Loss**: Many species will lose their habitats due to climate change-driven factors like desertification, deforestation, and sea-level rise. Arctic and alpine ecosystems, as well as coral reefs, are particularly vulnerable.
- **Coral Bleaching**: A 2°C increase would likely lead to widespread coral bleaching events, resulting in the decline or collapse of coral reefs, which support rich marine biodiversity and protect coastlines.
- **Species Extinctions**: As ecosystems shift faster than species can adapt, extinction rates will increase. Tropical rainforests, savannas, and polar regions are especially vulnerable to biodiversity loss.

2.4 Ocean Acidification and Marine Life Impacts

As global temperatures rise, the oceans absorb more carbon dioxide (CO_2), which causes ocean acidification. This has profound consequences:

- **Disruption of Marine Food Chains**: Ocean acidification affects marine organisms, especially those with calcium carbonate shells, such as mollusks, plankton, and corals. This threatens the entire marine food web.

- **Fishery Declines**: Many commercial fish species rely on coral reefs and plankton. The loss of these critical habitats and food sources could reduce fish populations, affecting global food security.

2.5 Permafrost Thaw and Methane Release

A temperature rise beyond 2°C will accelerate the thawing of permafrost, releasing large quantities of methane, a potent greenhouse gas:

- **Methane Feedback Loop**: The release of methane from thawing permafrost creates a feedback loop that amplifies warming, making it more difficult to limit temperature rise.
- **Disruption of Arctic Ecosystems**: Thawing permafrost disrupts ecosystems, causing the collapse of landscapes and affecting species such as reindeer, polar bears, and migratory birds that depend on these habitats.

2.6 Agriculture and Food Security

Higher global temperatures have a direct impact on agriculture:

- **Reduced Crop Yields**: Heat stress and shifting rainfall patterns will reduce crop yields, especially for staples like wheat, maize, and rice in tropical and temperate regions.
- **Soil Degradation**: Increased soil erosion, desertification, and salinization will further threaten global food production.
- **Fisheries and Livestock**: Changes in water temperature and chemistry will affect fish stocks, while heat stress will reduce livestock productivity.

2.7 Water Scarcity

Global warming beyond 2°C will exacerbate water scarcity in many regions:

- **Glacier Melt and Water Supply**: Many communities and agricultural areas rely on glacier-fed rivers. As glaciers retreat, freshwater availability will decrease, especially in regions such as South Asia and the Andes.
- **Shifting Precipitation Patterns**: More intense and erratic rainfall will result in water scarcity in regions already facing droughts, while other regions may experience excessive rainfall and flooding.

3. Social and Economic Consequences

The environmental impacts of exceeding 2°C will have profound social and economic ramifications:

- **Climate Refugees**: Rising sea levels, extreme weather, and degraded ecosystems could displace millions of people, creating climate refugees and exacerbating global conflicts over resources.
- **Public Health Threats**: The increased frequency of heatwaves, the spread of vector-borne diseases (like malaria and dengue), and the loss of clean water sources will pose significant public health challenges.
- **Economic Losses**: Climate change impacts on agriculture, fisheries, infrastructure, and health will lead to economic losses that disproportionately affect developing countries, while straining global trade and security.

Chapter One
Energy Basics

Kinds of Energy and Properties

Before we discuss the dynamics of the transition from fossil fuel to renewable energy it is important to understand some basic facts about energy. All energy on Earth comes from the sun. fossil fuel energy is the energy that fell on the earth hundreds of millions of years ago and was absorbed by plant life and stored it in carbon-based compounds while it was alive. When the plant life died it was buried in the ground. As a result of geological processes, carbon was concentrated into various forms such as coal petroleum and natural gas. Today the fossil fuel industry harvests this energy by extracting these minerals from the ground and in some cases like petroleum process them into various subcomponents to allow it to be used in various ways depending upon the energy requirements Such as gasoline for automobiles diesel for trucks heating oil etcetera.

On the other hand, renewable energy such as wind, solar, and hydroelectric capture the energy falling on the Earth today. Solar panels captured it directly and converted into electricity. Wind turbines capture the energy that results from uneven heating of the atmosphere, which causes flow from high pressure areas to low pressure areas. The wind turbine captures the wind energy and creates electric energy.. Hydroelectric power captures the energy from the evaporation process where water on the land or the sea evaporates, rises up into the atmosphere and then eventually condenses into rain. As gravity causes the water to flow back to the ocean hydroelectric turbines capture the gravitational energy as the waterfalls and converts it to electrical energy by a turbine.

The basic difference between fossil fuel energy and renewable energy is fossil fuels store energy for future use. They involve bulk which must be extracted processed and transported to the place where the energy is going to be consumed. Gasoline is an ideal fuel for automobiles because it has a high energy content relative to the bulk and weight of the material. Renewable energy such as solar panels and wind turbines create energy directly to electricity which must be used as soon as it's created or stored in batteries.

The generation of electricity from solar and wind depends upon the availability of sunshine and the intensity of wind. The electricity created by a hydroelectric turbine must also be used as soon as it's created. However, dams store up water in reservoirs which can be released to create electricity on a cycle that matches demand rather than when it is generated as a result of availability of sunlight or wind.

Hydroelectric power is the most efficient power.

Hydroelectric power was and still is the cheapest way of producing electrical energy because it utilizes facilities 24/7 and in most cases 365 while solar panels and wind turbines can only generate electricity when the sun is shining or the wind is blowing. Which can also vary in intensity during the time of the day and season.

The only limiting factor on hydroelectric is seasonal rainfall. Usually the greater amount of rainfall is in the winter months. It is stored behind dams and used during the summer months when demand for electricity is higher and the availability of water from rainfall is less.

An advantage of renewable energy is it is energy captured from the sun and delivered directly to the user through an infrastructure of power lines On the other hand electric vehicles are limited by the capacity of batteries to store enough energy to allow a driving range that is practical for varying transportation needs.

The advantage of renewable energy systems over fossil fuel systems is that they do not require any fuel. Once the infrastructure such as the solar panel wind turbine or hydroelectric dam are built ongoing cost are limited to cost of maintaining the infrastructure.

This is the reason why renewable energy is inherently cheaper than fossil fuels which must be transported and processed in some cases. In addition to the carbon dioxide methane which causes global warming fossil fuels often involve other contaminations such as nitrous oxide which have detrimental effects to the environment.

Generally, the major cost for renewable energy is in the construction and maintenance of the generating facility. Once the facility is built costs are minimal. On the other hand, in the case of fossil fuel generation an ongoing supply of fossil fuels is required to generate the electricity, so this results in an ongoing cost. Also, as we've experienced over the last few decades the price of fossil fuels can vary significantly thus making this cost very valuable and unpredictable at times. On the other hand, in the case of renewable energy once the facilities are built their cost is pretty much fixed until the asset is retired.

Thermodynamics

Thermodynamics is a branch of physics that studies the relationship between heat work temperature and energy focusing on how energy is transferred between systems and how it can be used to perform work governed by fundamental laws that describe the behavior of these quantities in a system including the concepts of entropy and internal energy essentially it examines how energy changes form and moves within a system with key applications in various scientific and engineering fields like chemistry mechanical engineering and biochemistry.

The keywords here are transforming heat into work. When I was in school, I was taught that the industrial revolution was enabled by standardized parts which allowed mass production. I don't remember ever being told that replacing human energy with energy from fossil fuels was as important or more important than standardized parts to the success of the industrial revolution. It is telling that the standard unit of measure in thermodynamics is horsepower. An engine is measured in its capacity do you produce energy in an equivalent number of horses.

The steam engine replaced the stagecoach, men on horseback, and horse drawn wagons. Ironically with steamboats the energy of a steam engine replaced the power of the wind, because steam engines provided more power and reliable power than the wind. Today some ships are being retrofitted so that the power of the main propulsion system which uses fossil fuels is enhanced by the power of the wind

In the following chapter we will examine how fossil fuels impacted on the industrial revolution over the last two centuries.

Chapter Two
The Impact of Fossil Fuels on the Development of the Industrial Revolution

The Industrial Revolution, which began in the late 18th century, marked a period of profound economic, social, and technological transformation. Central to this revolution was the increasing reliance on fossil fuels—coal, oil, and natural gas. These energy sources powered the rise of mechanized industries, revolutionized transportation, and reshaped global economies. This report provides an overview of how fossil fuels influenced the development of various industries, outlines the timeline of their increasing impact, and discusses the long-term consequences from 1800 to the present.

Early Industrial Revolution (1800-1850): The Rise of Coal

At the dawn of the Industrial Revolution, coal became the dominant source of energy, replacing traditional fuels like wood and biomass. Coal's high energy density made it a superior alternative for powering steam engines, which were crucial to the mechanization of industries. The following sectors were among the first to benefit from coal:

1. **Textile Industry:**
    - The introduction of steam-powered machinery, such as the spinning jenny and power loom, revolutionized

textile production. Factories grew larger and more efficient, leading to mass production of textiles.

- Coal-fired steam engines powered both machines and looms, enabling faster production with fewer human laborers.

2. **Iron and Steel Industry:**
   - Coal was essential in iron production, particularly through the use of blast furnaces that smelted iron ore more efficiently.
   - By 1850, the Bessemer process, which required vast amounts of coal to produce steel, made steel production cheaper and faster, fueling the expansion of railroads and construction industries.
3. **Transportation:**
   - The development of the steam engine, pioneered by James Watt, was powered by coal and applied to railways and shipping.
   - The first steam-powered locomotive was built in 1804, with railways rapidly expanding by the 1830s, transforming domestic and international trade.

Mid-Industrial Revolution (1850-1900): Oil Enters the Picture

While coal dominated the early stages of the Industrial Revolution, oil began to play a growing role in the late 19th century. The discovery of oil fields and the development of new technologies for oil extraction and refining laid the groundwork for a second wave of industrialization.

1. **Transportation:**
   - By the 1860s, kerosene, derived from oil, became widely used for lighting, replacing whale oil and reducing demand for coal in this domain.
   - In the 1880s, the invention of the internal combustion engine led to the development of automobiles. This marked the beginning of oil's dominance in the transportation sector, with gasoline and diesel engines gradually replacing steam engines.
2. **Chemical Industry:**
   - Oil refining led to the creation of petrochemical industries. By the late 19th century, oil-based products like lubricants, solvents, and synthetic dyes were in increasing demand.
   - Fossil fuels became a critical feedstock for chemical manufacturing, giving rise to a new array of industrial applications in fertilizers, plastics, and pharmaceuticals.

Early 20th Century (1900-1950): Oil and the Rise of Global Industry

The early 20th century marked the expansion of oil as a key energy source, coinciding with the development of new industries and transportation systems.

1. **Automotive Industry:**
   - The mass production of automobiles by companies like Ford in the early 20th century increased the demand for oil, especially for gasoline.

- By the 1920s, cars became more affordable, reshaping urban landscapes with roads, highways, and fuel stations.

2. **Aviation Industry:**
   - The Wright brothers' first flight in 1903, powered by an internal combustion engine, marked the beginning of the aviation age. Aircraft fuel requirements made oil a critical component of the expanding aerospace sector.

3. **Energy Generation:**
   - Although coal remained a major energy source for electricity generation, oil-powered generators became increasingly common. Hydroelectricity and the early exploration of natural gas also contributed to the growing diversification of energy sources.

Mid-20th Century to Late 20th Century (1950-2000): The Dominance of Oil and Natural Gas

After World War II, fossil fuels, particularly oil and natural gas, became central to the post-war economic boom, propelling industries to new heights.

1. **Energy and Electricity Generation:**
   - The 1950s and 1960s saw an increased reliance on oil and natural gas for electricity generation, with power plants rapidly switching from coal to oil and gas.
   - The nuclear energy boom of the 1970s offered a brief alternative, but fossil fuels remained the dominant source of global energy.

2. **Chemical and Petrochemical Industries:**
    - The widespread use of petrochemicals, derived from oil and natural gas, revolutionized consumer goods, giving rise to mass-produced plastics, synthetic fibers, and fertilizers.
    - The development of synthetic polymers (such as nylon and polyester) further enhanced the role of fossil fuels in everyday life.
3. **Global Transportation and Shipping:**
    - The rise of globalized trade in the late 20th century was fueled by oil-powered cargo ships, airplanes, and trucks.
    - International logistics systems became heavily dependent on fossil fuels for both shipping goods and maintaining supply chains across the world.

21st Century (2000-Present): Fossil Fuels, Environmental Awareness, and Transition

In the 21st century, the consequences of heavy fossil fuel reliance—climate change, air pollution, and environmental degradation—have sparked a global shift toward cleaner energy alternatives. However, fossil fuels continue to dominate many sectors.

1. **Energy and Climate Impact:**
    - In 2000, over 85% of the world's energy came from fossil fuels (oil, coal, and natural gas). Since then, renewables like wind and solar have seen significant growth, but fossil fuels still account for about 80% of global energy consumption.

- The burning of fossil fuels has become the leading contributor to greenhouse gas emissions, driving global warming and prompting international agreements like the Paris Agreement (2015) to reduce carbon emissions.

2. **Transition to Renewable Energy:**
   - While coal usage has declined in many developed countries, natural gas has remained a major energy source due to its lower carbon emissions compared to coal.
   - Oil consumption, particularly for transportation, remains high, although electric vehicles (EVs) are gaining momentum. Governments and industries worldwide are investing in renewable energy technologies such as solar, wind, and hydropower to reduce dependence on fossil fuels.

3. **Fossil Fuels and Industry Today:**
   - Industries like manufacturing, chemical production, and transportation still rely heavily on fossil fuels, though there is a shift toward sustainability in some sectors.
   - Despite global efforts, fossil fuels continue to play a critical role in the industrial economy, with the oil industry alone generating trillions in revenues annually.

Timeline of Fossil Fuel Impact (1800-Present)

- **1800-1850:** Coal revolutionizes the textile and iron industries; steam engines emerge as a key innovation.
- **1850-1900:** Oil enters the energy market, with early applications in lighting and transportation.
- **1900-1950:** Oil surpasses coal in importance, powering the automobile and aviation industries.
- **1950-2000:** Natural gas rises alongside oil; petrochemicals reshape consumer industries; global trade relies on fossil-fuel-powered transportation.
- **2000-Present:** Increasing awareness of climate change leads to a gradual shift toward renewable energy, although fossil fuels still dominate global energy consumption.

Conclusion

Fossil fuels were instrumental in fueling the growth of the Industrial Revolution and have continued to play a central role in modern industrialization. Coal, oil, and natural gas transformed industries like textiles, iron, steel, transportation, and energy generation. While these fuels enabled unprecedented economic development, their environmental impacts have become a significant global challenge, leading to current efforts to transition to cleaner, renewable energy sources.

Chapter Three
Global Impacts of the Demise of the Fossil Fuel Industry

1. Introduction

The decline of the fossil fuel industry is a significant event with profound economic, environmental, and geopolitical impacts worldwide. With the shift to renewable energy sources accelerating, countries heavily reliant on oil, coal, and natural gas face economic restructuring challenges, while others may benefit from cleaner, sustainable energy systems. This report assesses the impacts of the fossil fuel industry's demise by country, focusing on the economic, social, and geopolitical changes likely to occur and the projected timeline for these transitions.

2. Drivers of the Demise of the Fossil Fuel Industry

Several factors are accelerating the decline of the fossil fuel industry globally. These drivers are a mix of economic, environmental, technological, and policy-related factors, which together create an environment where fossil fuel demand is decreasing while renewable energy sources are gaining traction. Key drivers include:

A. Global Climate Change Policies

- **International Agreements:** The 2015 Paris Agreement marked a turning point in global climate policy. Nearly 200 countries committed to limiting global warming to well below 2°C, with ambitions to keep it under 1.5°C. This requires significant reductions in greenhouse gas (GHG) emissions, which are primarily driven by the burning of fossil fuels. The pressure to meet these targets has led to stronger environmental regulations and commitments to transition to low-carbon energy systems.

- **National Carbon Policies:** Many countries are implementing carbon pricing mechanisms, emissions trading systems, and carbon taxes to penalize fossil fuel use. For instance, the European Union's Emissions Trading System (EU ETS) and Canada's carbon tax have already made fossil fuels less attractive compared to renewables.

B. Technological Advancements in Renewable Energy

- **Cost Parity:** The cost of renewable energy technologies, particularly solar photovoltaics (PV) and wind turbines has dropped dramatically over the past decade. According to the International Renewable Energy Agency (IRENA), the cost of solar electricity fell by over 80% between 2010 and 2020, while wind energy costs fell by 40%. Many renewables have now reached cost parity with fossil fuels, making them economically competitive without subsidies.
- **Energy Storage Advancements:** Breakthroughs in battery storage technology are addressing the intermittent nature of renewables like solar and wind. Lithium-ion battery costs have dropped significantly, enabling more reliable renewable energy grids. This is also driving the electrification of transport, reducing the need for fossil fuels in the automotive sector.

- **Hydrogen and Other Emerging Technologies:** Green hydrogen, produced through electrolysis powered by renewables, offers potential for decarbonizing sectors that are difficult to electrify, such as heavy industry and aviation. Innovations in carbon capture and storage (CCS) and nuclear energy also contribute to reducing reliance on fossil fuels.

C. Economic Pressures and Fossil Fuel Volatility

- **Price Volatility:** Fossil fuel markets, especially oil, are historically volatile. Price fluctuations, often driven by geopolitical events, supply disruptions, or shifts in global demand, make fossil fuels an uncertain foundation for long-term economic planning. For example, oil price crashes in 2014 and 2020 exposed the vulnerability of oil-dependent economies.

- **Divestment Movement:** Institutional investors are increasingly divesting from fossil fuel companies due to both financial risk and growing social pressure. Pension funds, universities, and sovereign wealth funds are pulling out of fossil fuel investments, with trillions of dollars already divested. This trend is reinforced by the growing perception that fossil fuel assets may become "stranded" as the world transitions to cleaner energy sources.

- **Fossil Fuel Extraction Costs:** The costs associated with extracting fossil fuels, especially from unconventional sources like deepwater or shale, are high compared to the continually decreasing costs of renewable energy generation. This makes further investments in fossil fuel infrastructure less attractive.

D. Electrification of Transportation

- **Rise of Electric Vehicles (EVs):** The global automotive industry is undergoing a rapid transition from internal combustion engine (ICE) vehicles to electric vehicles. Major automakers, including Tesla, General Motors, and Volkswagen, have announced plans to phase out ICE vehicles in favor of electric ones. As EV adoption increases, oil demand for transportation is expected to fall significantly. According to BloombergNEF, EVs could account for 54% of new car sales by 2040.

- **Government Support for EVs:** Governments around the world are providing incentives for EV adoption through subsidies, tax breaks, and infrastructure development (e.g., charging stations). Countries like Norway, the UK, and China are leading the way, with some planning to ban sales of new fossil fuel-powered vehicles by the 2030s.

E. Corporate Commitments to Sustainability

- **Net-Zero Pledges:** Many of the world's largest corporations, including those in energy-intensive sectors, have made commitments to achieve net-zero emissions by mid-century. These companies are investing heavily in renewable energy, electrification, and energy efficiency to meet these goals. Major oil and gas companies, such as BP, Shell, and TotalEnergies, have also shifted their strategies, investing in renewable energy, carbon capture, and hydrogen projects.
- **Supply Chain Pressure:** Multinational corporations are increasingly requiring their suppliers to reduce carbon emissions, which puts further pressure on fossil fuel consumption. Large corporations like Apple, Amazon, and Unilever are pushing for greener supply chains, which in turn creates demand for renewable energy across various industries.

F. Consumer Preferences and Social Movements

- **Public Demand for Clean Energy:** There is growing public awareness of climate change, leading to increased consumer demand for clean energy and sustainable products. This shift is affecting markets globally, from the demand for electric vehicles to renewable energy for households. The rise of environmental, social, and governance (ESG) criteria in investment decisions further supports the transition.

- **Youth and Climate Activism:** Movements like Fridays for Future, led by young climate activists like Greta Thunberg, have drawn global attention to the urgent need to act on climate change. Public pressure, especially from younger generations, is influencing political decisions and corporate behavior in favor of decarbonization.

G. Global Supply Chain and Energy Security Shifts

- **Supply Chain Diversification:** Countries and businesses are looking to reduce their dependence on fossil fuels due to supply chain vulnerabilities exposed by geopolitical conflicts (e.g., Russia-Ukraine war). Governments are seeking to diversify energy sources and reduce reliance on imported fossil fuels, driving investments in local renewable energy production.

- **Energy Independence:** Renewable energy offers the possibility of energy independence for many countries. Wind, solar, and hydropower can be locally generated, reducing reliance on imports from fossil-fuel-rich nations and increasing national energy security. This shift is especially important in the European Union, Japan, and other regions dependent on imported energy.

3. Conclusion

The demise of the fossil fuel industry is driven by a convergence of environmental policies, technological advancements, economic pressures, and shifting societal values. These factors are reshaping global energy markets, forcing fossil fuel companies to adapt or face decline. The combination of climate policies, the falling costs of renewables, electrification of transport, and changing consumer preferences suggests that the fossil fuel industry's contraction will continue in the coming decades, with significant global impacts.

3. Countries Most Affected by the Decline of Fossil Fuels

The global shift away from fossil fuels will have disproportionate effects on countries based on their dependence on oil, gas, and coal production and exports. Countries with economies heavily reliant on fossil fuels face challenges in restructuring their economies, managing social impacts, and navigating geopolitical shifts. The following section analyzes the countries most affected by the decline of fossil fuels.

A. Saudi Arabia

1. Economic Impact

Saudi Arabia's economy is deeply tied to oil revenues, making it one of the most vulnerable nations to the global shift away from fossil fuels. Oil exports contribute approximately 60% of the Kingdom's government revenues, over 40% of its GDP, and account for around 75% of its total exports. Consequently, any significant drop in global demand for oil will result in:

- **Government Revenue Losses:** A sustained decline in oil prices and demand will lead to budget deficits, limiting the government's ability to fund key projects, social services, and subsidies.

- **Investment Constraints:** The loss of oil revenue will affect Saudi Arabia's ability to invest in its ambitious Vision 2030, a development program aimed at diversifying the economy. The Kingdom's Public Investment Fund (PIF), which is heavily financed by oil profits, will face challenges in supporting domestic industries such as technology, tourism, and entertainment.

- **Debt Levels:** Saudi Arabia could increase its reliance on international debt markets to finance its budget, leading to higher levels of public debt, potentially eroding the financial stability it has enjoyed due to its vast oil reserves.

2. Diversification Efforts (Vision 2030)

Saudi Arabia's leadership, recognizing its dependence on fossil fuels, has launched **Vision 2030**, a comprehensive plan to diversify its economy. Key goals of the initiative include:

- **Developing Non-Oil Sectors:** The Kingdom is investing in sectors such as tourism, entertainment, renewable energy, technology, and manufacturing. Projects like NEOM, a $500 billion mega-city, are part of the strategy to attract foreign investment and reduce dependence on oil.

- **Privatization and Foreign Investment:** The government has begun to privatize state-owned assets, such as selling shares of Saudi Aramco, to raise capital for diversification efforts.

- **Renewable Energy Initiatives:** Saudi Arabia is investing in solar and wind energy to not only diversify its energy mix but also establish itself as a global leader in green energy exports. One key project is the development of a large-scale green hydrogen plant in NEOM, positioning the Kingdom as a future supplier of clean fuels.

However, these diversification efforts face challenges. The pace of global energy transition may outstrip Saudi Arabia's ability to successfully transform its economy in time to replace oil revenues, making the 2030 timeline ambitious.

3. Timeline for Impact

Saudi Arabia's economy could start to feel the impacts of declining fossil fuel demand as early as **2025**, with significant effects anticipated by **2030**. The following are projected milestones:

- **2025:** Global oil demand may reach a peak, followed by a gradual decline due to increasing adoption of electric vehicles (EVs) and renewable energy in major markets like the European Union, China, and the United States.
- **2025-2030:** As international climate policies become more aggressive, oil prices could become increasingly volatile, creating financial strain. The Kingdom's ability to finance public projects and maintain subsidies may be challenged.
- **2030 and Beyond:** By 2030, Saudi Arabia could face a prolonged period of budget deficits if oil prices do not recover. The success of Vision 2030 will become critical, but if diversification efforts falter, the Kingdom may struggle to stabilize its economy.

4. Geopolitical Impact

Saudi Arabia's geopolitical influence has long been tied to its vast oil reserves and its leadership within the Organization of the Petroleum Exporting Countries (OPEC). As the global reliance on oil diminishes:

- **OPEC Influence:** The power of OPEC, and by extension Saudi Arabia's influence over global oil prices, will weaken. Major oil-importing regions like the EU and China are accelerating their energy independence, reducing the need for OPEC's role in stabilizing oil markets.

- **Regional Shifts:** The decline in oil revenues could lead to a reshuffling of regional power dynamics in the Middle East. Saudi Arabia may face increased competition from countries like the UAE and Qatar, which have diversified their economies more successfully.
- **Military and Foreign Policy:** With a reduction in oil revenue, Saudi Arabia's capacity to engage in costly foreign policy activities, such as its involvement in Yemen, may be curtailed. Economic constraints could also reduce the Kingdom's ability to exert influence through foreign aid and investment.

5. Social Impact

The decline of fossil fuels will have significant social consequences for Saudi Arabia, where a large proportion of the population is employed directly or indirectly by the oil industry:

- **Job Losses:** The contraction of the oil sector may lead to widespread unemployment, especially in regions dependent on fossil fuel production and related industries. While Vision 2030 aims to create new jobs in non-oil sectors, the pace of transition may not be sufficient to absorb displaced workers.
- **Social Stability:** Oil revenues have long financed the Kingdom’s generous social welfare programs and subsidies. Budget cuts or austerity measures could lead to social discontent, particularly among the youth, who make up a large part of the population.
- **Cultural Shifts:** Vision 2030 seeks to liberalize the Saudi economy and reduce dependence on government handouts. This could lead to social changes, including greater private

sector participation and a shift toward a more entrepreneurial society. However, it may also create tensions as citizens adjust to a new economic reality where oil wealth is no longer the primary source of prosperity.

6. Conclusion

Saudi Arabia stands at a critical juncture in its economic history. The decline of global oil demand will have profound economic, social, and geopolitical impacts on the Kingdom. While the government's Vision 2030 offers a pathway toward diversification and modernization, the rapid pace of the global energy transition poses significant risks. The country's ability to successfully navigate this transition will depend on its capacity to create new industries, attract foreign investment, and manage the social and economic impacts of reduced oil revenues. The next decade will be crucial in determining whether Saudi Arabia can adapt to a post-oil world.

B. Russia

1. Economic Impact

Russia is one of the world's largest oil and natural gas exporters, with fossil fuels accounting for a significant portion of its economy. Key economic impacts of the decline in fossil fuel demand include:

- **Revenue Dependence:** Oil and gas exports contribute approximately 40% of the Russian federal budget, and around 60% of total exports. A sustained decline in fossil fuel prices and demand could lead to severe budget deficits, restricting government spending on public services and infrastructure.
- **GDP Contraction:** The Russian economy is highly vulnerable to fluctuations in global energy prices. For example, the International Monetary Fund (IMF) estimated that a 10% decrease in oil prices could reduce GDP by 2%. If

global demand decreases significantly, Russia could face prolonged economic stagnation or recession.

- **Investment Declines:** Foreign investments in the Russian energy sector may decline as international companies reduce their exposure to fossil fuels. Major Western oil companies, such as BP and ExxonMobil, have already begun to withdraw from Russian operations due to sanctions and shifting market dynamics.

2. Geopolitical Impact

Russia's geopolitical power has historically been bolstered by its vast energy resources, which it uses as a tool for influence, especially in Europe. However, the decline of fossil fuels will have significant geopolitical ramifications:

- **Energy Leverage Erosion:** Russia has relied on its energy exports to exert influence over European nations. As the EU aggressively transitions to renewable energy and diversifies its gas supplies (e.g., importing liquefied natural gas from the U.S. and Qatar), Russia's leverage over Europe will diminish, reducing its political influence in the region.

- **Changing Alliances:** The global energy transition could lead to a reevaluation of alliances. Countries in Europe and Asia may seek to strengthen ties with energy producers focused on renewable sources, sidelining Russia as an energy partner.

- **Military Spending Constraints:** The decline in oil revenues may force the Russian government to cut military spending, impacting its ability to project power abroad and maintain its military presence in regions like Ukraine and Syria.

3. Domestic Challenges

The economic and geopolitical shifts resulting from the decline of fossil fuels will lead to several domestic challenges:

- **Social Unrest:** Economic hardship caused by reduced government revenue could lead to social unrest, particularly among populations dependent on the energy sector. Public dissatisfaction could grow if the government struggles to maintain social services, pensions, and employment in energy-dependent regions.
- **Regional Disparities:** Regions heavily reliant on fossil fuel extraction, such as Siberia, may experience significant economic decline, leading to increased regional inequalities and tensions. This could drive migration to urban areas, exacerbating social issues in cities.
- **Political Stability:** Economic challenges could undermine public support for the current regime. President Vladimir Putin's administration has historically relied on the economy's stability to maintain political power. If economic conditions deteriorate significantly, the potential for political instability may increase.

4. Environmental Considerations

The decline of the fossil fuel industry offers some potential environmental benefits for Russia:

- **Reduced Emissions:** As the world moves toward cleaner energy sources, Russia's carbon emissions could decrease significantly. This transition presents an opportunity for the country to reduce its environmental impact and participate in global efforts to combat climate change.

- **Biodiversity Protection:** Reducing fossil fuel extraction may benefit Russia's vast and sensitive ecosystems, particularly in Siberia and the Arctic, where oil and gas development poses significant environmental risks.
- **Sustainable Development Initiatives:** The government may be compelled to invest in renewable energy sources and sustainable development initiatives, which could create jobs and foster a greener economy.

5. Transition Strategies

To mitigate the economic and social impacts of fossil fuel decline, Russia may consider several strategies:

- **Diversification Efforts:** The government will need to develop a roadmap for economic diversification to reduce dependence on fossil fuel revenues. This could include investments in technology, agriculture, and tourism, as well as support for small and medium-sized enterprises.
- **Renewable Energy Investments:** Russia possesses substantial renewable energy resources, particularly in wind and hydropower. Investing in these sectors can help create new economic opportunities and reduce reliance on fossil fuels.
- **International Cooperation:** Engaging in international climate agreements and cooperating with other nations on renewable energy projects could help Russia adapt to the changing energy landscape while maintaining its role in the global economy.

6. Conclusion

The decline of the fossil fuel industry poses significant challenges for Russia, a country whose economy and geopolitical influence are heavily reliant on oil and gas exports. The potential for revenue losses, economic contraction, and social unrest could lead to profound changes within the country. To navigate this transition successfully, Russia will need to prioritize economic diversification, invest in renewable energy, and address the social implications of declining fossil fuel revenues. The path forward will require significant adjustments, both domestically and internationally, as the country adapts to a rapidly changing global energy landscape.

C. Venezuela

1. Economic Impact

Venezuela is home to the world's largest proven oil reserves, making it highly dependent on oil revenues. However, years of political instability, mismanagement, and economic sanctions have led to a catastrophic decline in its oil industry, which now faces even further challenges due to the global shift away from fossil fuels. Key economic impacts include:

- **Revenue Decline:** Oil exports accounted for approximately 90% of Venezuela's total exports and around 40% of GDP before the industry began to collapse. The continuing decline in global oil demand, compounded by sanctions, is likely to lead to an exacerbation of the country's already dire financial situation.

- **Hyperinflation and Economic Collapse:** Venezuela has been experiencing hyperinflation for several years, with the economy contracting by an estimated 80% since 2013. The loss of oil revenue will intensify the current economic collapse, leading to increased inflation and greater poverty levels.

- **Foreign Investment Exit:** International companies are hesitant to invest in Venezuela due to political risks and the deteriorating economic situation. The exit of foreign investment will limit the country's ability to revive its oil industry and diversify its economy.

2. Social Impact

The economic collapse has had devastating social consequences for the Venezuelan population:

- **Humanitarian Crisis:** Venezuela is currently facing one of the worst humanitarian crises in the world, with millions experiencing food shortages, lack of medical care, and deteriorating living conditions. The decline of the oil industry will worsen this crisis, leading to increased malnutrition and preventable diseases.
- **Mass Migration:** The ongoing economic collapse has triggered a mass exodus of Venezuelans seeking better opportunities abroad. Over 7 million people have left the country since 2014, primarily to neighboring countries in Latin America. This outflow could increase as conditions deteriorate further.
- **Increased Unemployment:** The contraction of the oil sector will lead to further job losses, worsening the already high unemployment rate. The loss of income for families will exacerbate the economic hardships they face.

3. Geopolitical Impact

Venezuela's geopolitical situation is also affected by the decline of the fossil fuel industry:

- **Declining Influence in OPEC:** Venezuela is a founding member of the Organization of the Petroleum Exporting Countries (OPEC), but its declining production capacity reduces its influence within the organization. OPEC's efforts to stabilize oil prices may be less impactful with a weaker Venezuelan presence.

- **Strained Relations with Allies:** The decline in oil revenues can also impact Venezuela's relationships with allies that benefit from its oil exports, such as China and Russia. These countries may reevaluate their support as Venezuela's economic viability diminishes.
- **Potential for Instability:** The political crisis in Venezuela has the potential to destabilize the region. As the economy collapses, social unrest may grow, leading to political instability that could affect neighboring countries and increase regional tensions.

4. Environmental Considerations

The decline of the fossil fuel industry might also lead to some environmental benefits, though these come amidst ongoing challenges:

- **Reduced Pollution:** A decrease in oil production could reduce the environmental degradation associated with oil extraction, including air and water pollution. However, the ongoing environmental damage from past oil spills and improper extraction practices will require significant remediation efforts.
- **Biodiversity Threats:** Venezuela's rich biodiversity is threatened by the oil industry, especially in the Orinoco Belt region. The decline of fossil fuels may provide an opportunity to focus on conservation efforts, but the government will need to prioritize environmental protection over immediate economic recovery.

- **Green Energy Potential:** While Venezuela has immense oil reserves, it also has significant renewable energy potential, especially in hydropower and solar energy. Investing in renewable energy could create jobs and help diversify the economy, but current conditions limit the feasibility of such projects.

5. Transition Strategies

To mitigate the adverse effects of declining fossil fuel revenues, Venezuela may need to adopt several strategies:

- **Economic Diversification:** The government must develop a comprehensive plan to diversify the economy away from oil dependence. This could involve investing in agriculture, tourism, and other sectors to create alternative sources of revenue and employment.
- **International Support and Cooperation:** Venezuela will need international assistance to stabilize its economy and address the humanitarian crisis. Rebuilding diplomatic relations and seeking support from international organizations could be crucial for recovery efforts.
- **Focus on Renewable Energy:** Despite the challenges, there is potential for Venezuela to invest in renewable energy sources, particularly solar and wind, to establish a more sustainable energy future. However, this will require investment, infrastructure development, and a stable political environment.

6. Conclusion

Venezuela's heavy reliance on fossil fuels has left it vulnerable to significant economic, social, and geopolitical challenges. The decline of the oil industry exacerbates an already dire humanitarian crisis and could lead to greater instability in the region. To navigate this transition successfully, Venezuela must focus on economic diversification, rebuilding international relations, and addressing the immediate needs of its population. The future of Venezuela will depend on its ability to adapt to a post-oil world and invest in sustainable alternatives that can provide long-term stability and growth.

D. Nigeria

1. Economic Impact

Nigeria is one of the largest oil producers in Africa, and its economy is heavily reliant on oil exports, which account for approximately 90% of total export revenues and about 60% of government revenues. The decline of the fossil fuel industry poses several economic challenges:

- **Revenue Vulnerability:** As global demand for oil decreases, Nigeria's federal budget, which heavily relies on oil revenues, will face significant shortfalls. This could lead to austerity measures and cuts to public services, exacerbating existing economic challenges.
- **Economic Growth Slowdown:** The Nigerian economy has struggled with high unemployment rates and inflation. The decline in oil prices and demand could further inhibit growth, potentially pushing the economy into recession.
- **Investment Decline:** The uncertainty surrounding the future of the fossil fuel industry may deter foreign investment. Oil companies may reduce their operations or exit Nigeria, leading to further job losses and a decrease in local economic activity.

2. Social Impact

The decline of the fossil fuel sector will have profound social consequences for Nigeria:

- **Increased Poverty:** With reduced government revenue and economic contraction, many Nigerians could fall deeper into poverty. The World Bank estimates that over 40% of the population already lives below the poverty line, and this figure may rise as job opportunities dwindle.

- **Social Unrest:** Nigeria has a history of social unrest, often fueled by economic challenges. The decline in the oil sector could lead to increased protests and civil discontent, especially in oil-producing regions like the Niger Delta, where communities have long felt marginalized by the wealth generated from their resources.

- **Health and Education Crises:** Cuts in government spending could affect critical sectors such as health care and education. This would further degrade living conditions, leading to increased mortality rates and decreased educational attainment among the youth.

3. Geopolitical Impact

Nigeria's position in the global energy landscape is also affected by the decline of fossil fuels:

- **OPEC Membership Implications:** As a member of the Organization of the Petroleum Exporting Countries (OPEC), Nigeria has historically played a significant role in influencing oil prices. However, as global demand declines, Nigeria's influence within OPEC may diminish, particularly if it struggles to meet production quotas due to infrastructural challenges and funding constraints.

- **Regional Power Dynamics:** Nigeria has been viewed as a regional leader in West Africa, but the decline in oil revenues could impact its ability to exert influence and provide support to neighboring countries, particularly in security and economic matters.
- **Security Concerns:** The oil-producing regions of Nigeria, particularly the Niger Delta, have experienced significant unrest and violence related to oil extraction. As the economy contracts and livelihoods diminish, the potential for increased violence and instability in these regions may rise, threatening national security.

4. Environmental Considerations

The decline of the fossil fuel industry in Nigeria could present both challenges and opportunities for environmental sustainability:

- **Pollution and Environmental Damage:** The oil industry has historically contributed to significant environmental degradation in Nigeria, particularly in the Niger Delta region. Reduced oil production may lessen pollution levels, but existing damage requires ongoing remediation efforts.
- **Renewable Energy Potential:** Nigeria has substantial potential for renewable energy, especially in solar and hydropower. The decline of fossil fuels may prompt the government to invest in these sectors as a means of diversifying the economy and improving energy access for the population.
- **Climate Change Mitigation:** The transition to renewable energy could position Nigeria to play a role in global efforts to combat climate change. The government could focus on reducing its carbon footprint and contributing to international climate agreements.

5. Transition Strategies

To mitigate the negative impacts of declining fossil fuel revenues, Nigeria may need to pursue several strategies:

- **Economic Diversification:** Nigeria must prioritize diversifying its economy beyond oil. Investments in agriculture, manufacturing, and technology can create jobs and alternative sources of revenue.
- **Strengthening Governance and Institutions:** Improving governance, reducing corruption, and enhancing institutional capacity will be crucial for attracting foreign investment and implementing effective economic policies.
- **Investment in Renewable Energy:** The government should leverage Nigeria's abundant renewable energy resources to develop a sustainable energy sector, which could provide reliable power and reduce reliance on fossil fuels.
- **Community Engagement:** Engaging local communities in decision-making processes related to resource extraction and environmental management is essential for promoting social stability and ensuring equitable distribution of benefits.

6. Conclusion

Nigeria's heavy dependence on fossil fuels makes it highly vulnerable to the global decline of the oil industry. Economic, social, and geopolitical challenges will arise as the country grapples with reduced revenues and increased instability. To navigate this transition successfully, Nigeria must focus on economic diversification, invest in renewable energy, and strengthen governance. The future of Nigeria will depend on its ability to adapt to a changing global energy landscape and prioritize the well-being of its citizens.

E. United States

1. Economic Impact

The United States is one of the largest producers and consumers of fossil fuels in the world. The economic implications of the decline in the fossil fuel industry are complex and multifaceted:

- **Job Losses in the Fossil Fuel Sector:** The fossil fuel industry employs hundreds of thousands of workers in various capacities, including extraction, refining, and transportation. A significant decline in demand for oil and gas could lead to job losses in these sectors, impacting families and communities reliant on fossil fuel employment.

- **Shifts in Investment:** As investors pivot towards renewable energy sources, traditional fossil fuel companies may experience reduced capital inflows. This shift could lead to a decline in the stock prices of major oil and gas companies, impacting pension funds and investors dependent on energy sector performance.

- **Energy Prices Volatility:** The transition away from fossil fuels may lead to short-term volatility in energy prices, particularly if supply chains are disrupted or if there is an abrupt shift in energy consumption patterns. Consumers could face higher prices for energy in the transition phase.

- **Economic Growth Opportunities:** The decline of fossil fuels presents opportunities for growth in the renewable energy sector, which has been expanding rapidly. Job creation in solar, wind, and other renewable technologies may offset some losses in fossil fuel employment.

2. Social Impact

The social implications of declining fossil fuel dependence in the United States will vary across different regions:

- **Rural vs. Urban Disparities:** Many rural areas, particularly in states like Texas, North Dakota, and Wyoming, heavily depend on fossil fuel extraction for economic stability. The decline of the fossil fuel industry could exacerbate economic disparities between rural and urban areas, leading to population decline in affected regions.
- **Energy Transition Challenges:** Communities that rely on fossil fuel jobs may face challenges in transitioning to new industries. Adequate retraining programs and support for displaced workers will be crucial to mitigate social unrest and economic decline.
- **Environmental Justice:** Communities located near fossil fuel extraction sites often experience health risks and environmental degradation. The decline of the fossil fuel industry could lead to improved public health outcomes in these areas, but disparities in access to clean energy and economic opportunities must be addressed to ensure equitable outcomes.

3. Geopolitical Impact

The geopolitical implications of the U.S. transition away from fossil fuels are significant:

- **Energy Independence:** The United States has become increasingly energy independent due to its domestic oil and gas production. A decline in fossil fuel reliance could lead to shifts in energy trade dynamics, impacting relationships with major oil-producing nations.

- **Global Leadership in Renewables:** The U.S. could enhance its geopolitical standing by becoming a leader in renewable energy technology and climate change mitigation. This leadership role could strengthen alliances with countries prioritizing sustainability and environmental protection.
- **Impact on International Oil Markets:** A significant reduction in U.S. oil and gas consumption could alter global oil prices and trade flows, affecting countries that rely on oil exports. Nations like Saudi Arabia, Russia, and Venezuela may experience economic disruptions as demand shifts.

4. Environmental Considerations

The decline of the fossil fuel industry presents significant environmental opportunities and challenges for the United States:

- **Reduced Greenhouse Gas Emissions:** The transition away from fossil fuels is essential for meeting climate targets. A reduction in fossil fuel consumption could lead to significant declines in greenhouse gas emissions, contributing to global efforts to combat climate change.
- **Investment in Clean Energy:** The U.S. has the potential to invest heavily in renewable energy sources, such as solar, wind, and hydropower. Transitioning to a cleaner energy grid can lead to reduced pollution, improved air quality, and enhanced public health.
- **Infrastructure Resilience:** The shift from fossil fuels may necessitate substantial investment in infrastructure, including grid modernization and electric vehicle charging stations. Ensuring resilience in energy infrastructure will be vital to support the transition.

5. Transition Strategies

To navigate the decline of the fossil fuel industry effectively, the United States may adopt several strategies:

- **Support for Retraining Programs:** Developing programs to retrain workers displaced by the decline of the fossil fuel industry will be critical. This includes investing in education and job training in renewable energy sectors.
- **Federal and State Policy Support:** Policymakers must create an environment conducive to renewable energy investment, including incentives for clean energy development, tax credits for renewable projects, and support for research and development.
- **Public-Private Partnerships:** Collaborations between government entities and private companies can accelerate the transition to a clean energy economy. Investing in innovation and technology development will be essential to achieving energy goals.
- **Community Engagement:** Engaging communities in the planning and implementation of energy transition strategies will ensure that the voices of those most affected by the decline of fossil fuels are heard, fostering social cohesion and equitable outcomes.

6. Conclusion

The decline of the fossil fuel industry in the United States presents significant economic, social, and geopolitical challenges, but it also opens opportunities for growth in renewable energy and sustainable development. To navigate this transition successfully, the U.S. must focus on worker retraining, infrastructure investment, and community engagement. By embracing renewable energy and prioritizing environmental sustainability, the United States can position itself as a leader in the global energy transition while addressing the impacts on communities reliant on fossil fuel economies. The next decade will be critical in shaping the future of energy in the U.S. and its role in the global landscape.

F. Norway

1. Economic Impact

Norway is a significant player in the global oil and gas market, with fossil fuels accounting for approximately 20% of its GDP and over 40% of its export revenues. The decline of the fossil fuel industry presents both challenges and opportunities for the Norwegian economy:

- **Revenue Dependence:** The Norwegian government heavily relies on oil revenues to fund its extensive welfare state and public services. A sustained decline in global fossil fuel demand and prices could lead to budget deficits, necessitating cuts to public spending and social services.
- **Economic Diversification:** Norway has actively pursued policies to diversify its economy away from oil dependency through investments in technology, maritime industries, and renewable energy. The ongoing transition may accelerate these efforts, fostering innovation in non-oil sectors.
- **Investment in Renewable Energy:** Norway has the potential to become a leader in renewable energy, particularly in hydropower and offshore wind. The decline of the fossil fuel industry could spur increased investment in these sectors, creating new jobs and opportunities.

2. Social Impact

The social implications of the decline in the fossil fuel industry in Norway will vary across different demographics and regions:

- **Job Losses in Oil and Gas:** The fossil fuel sector employs a significant number of Norwegians, particularly in regions like Stavanger and Northern Norway. Job losses in this sector could lead to economic hardship for affected communities and may require comprehensive retraining programs for workers transitioning to new industries.
- **Equity Considerations:** Norway has historically benefited from a strong social safety net funded by oil revenues. A decline in these revenues may put pressure on social programs and create disparities in access to services, particularly in rural areas dependent on the oil industry.
- **Increased Focus on Sustainability:** As Norway transitions away from fossil fuels, there may be a stronger emphasis on sustainability and environmental responsibility in societal norms, influencing consumer behavior and public policy.

3. Geopolitical Impact

Norway's geopolitical position is influenced by its status as a major oil and gas exporter, particularly to Europe:

- **Energy Transition Leadership:** Norway has the opportunity to take a leading role in Europe's energy transition, particularly in providing renewable energy and technological expertise in green energy solutions.
- **Impact on European Energy Security:** As a major supplier of natural gas to Europe, a decline in Norway's fossil fuel production could impact European energy security, particularly as countries seek alternatives to Russian gas. This

shift could lead to increased investments in renewable energy partnerships with Norway.

- **Regional Cooperation:** Norway's commitment to climate goals may strengthen its ties with other Nordic countries and EU nations, fostering collaboration on renewable energy projects and climate initiatives.

4. Environmental Considerations

The decline of the fossil fuel industry in Norway may yield significant environmental benefits:

- **Reduced Emissions:** A decrease in oil and gas production will contribute to lower greenhouse gas emissions, helping Norway meet its climate commitments under international agreements such as the Paris Accord.
- **Biodiversity and Ecosystem Protection:** The reduction of fossil fuel extraction could help preserve Norway's natural landscapes and biodiversity, particularly in sensitive areas like the Arctic. Conservation efforts may become more feasible as attention shifts toward sustainability.
- **Investment in Green Technologies:** Norway's focus on developing and exporting green technologies, such as carbon capture and storage (CCS) and offshore wind, positions it as a potential leader in the global clean energy market.

5. Transition Strategies

To effectively manage the decline of the fossil fuel industry, Norway may pursue several strategies:

- **Economic Diversification Initiatives:** The government should continue to invest in sectors such as technology, renewable energy, and sustainable fisheries to reduce reliance on oil and gas revenues.

- **Education and Workforce Training:** Investing in education and retraining programs for workers in fossil fuel industries will be crucial in helping them transition to jobs in emerging sectors, particularly in renewable energy and technology.
- **Policy Frameworks for Sustainability:** Implementing policies that support renewable energy development, carbon reduction targets, and sustainable practices across industries will facilitate a smooth transition to a low-carbon economy.
- **Public Engagement and Transparency:** Engaging the public in discussions about the transition from fossil fuels, including the impacts on communities and the environment, will be vital in fostering support and ensuring equitable outcomes.

6. Conclusion

Norway's reliance on the fossil fuel industry presents significant challenges as global demand declines. However, the country is well-positioned to leverage its resources and expertise to lead in the transition to renewable energy. By focusing on economic diversification, investing in education and technology, and fostering public engagement, Norway can navigate the impacts of declining fossil fuel dependence while contributing to global sustainability efforts. The next decade will be crucial for Norway as it transitions toward a greener, more sustainable future.

G. Canada

1. Economic Impact

Canada is one of the world's largest oil and natural gas producers, with fossil fuels playing a major role in its economy. The decline of the fossil fuel industry will impact Canada's economy on several fronts:

- **Revenue Decline:** Oil and gas exports represent a significant portion of Canada's GDP, particularly in oil-rich provinces like Alberta. A sustained drop in global fossil fuel demand would reduce government revenues, affecting federal and provincial budgets and potentially leading to cuts in public services and infrastructure investment.

- **Regional Economic Disparities:** Canada's oil and gas industry is concentrated in Alberta, Saskatchewan, and Newfoundland and Labrador. The economic strain in these provinces could deepen regional disparities, potentially affecting interprovincial relations and placing strain on national unity.

- **Growth Opportunities in Clean Technology:** Canada's clean technology sector has been growing, and the shift away from fossil fuels could drive further investment in renewables, including hydropower, solar, wind, and biofuels, as well as emerging technologies like carbon capture and storage (CCS).

2. Social Impact

The decline of fossil fuels will have varying social implications across Canada, with notable impacts in oil-producing regions:

- **Job Losses in Oil and Gas:** The fossil fuel industry provides high-paying jobs in Canada, and its decline could lead to significant job losses, especially in regions like Alberta. This may lead to outmigration from these provinces and place further strain on families and communities reliant on oil-related employment.

- **Inequities in Transition:** Indigenous communities and rural areas involved in fossil fuel extraction may face unique challenges in the transition. For Indigenous communities that rely on fossil fuel projects for economic benefits, a decline could lead to financial hardship without equitable access to alternative opportunities.
- **Health and Environment Benefits:** As fossil fuel operations decline, communities may see reductions in air and water pollution, leading to improved public health. This shift will also allow for expanded focus on sustainability, energy efficiency, and climate resilience across Canada's social systems.

3. Geopolitical Impact

Canada's role as an oil exporter, particularly to the United States, affects its geopolitical positioning:

- **U.S.-Canada Energy Relations:** Canada exports a significant portion of its oil and gas to the United States, and a decline in demand may affect this critical trade relationship. However, both nations' shared focus on environmental goals could foster partnerships in clean energy.
- **Global Climate Leadership:** Canada has committed to achieving net-zero emissions by 2050. By reducing its reliance on fossil fuels, Canada can strengthen its standing as a leader in global climate policy, reinforcing alliances with countries pursuing similar sustainability goals.
- **Shift in Global Trade Patterns:** With a reduction in fossil fuel exports, Canada may increase its involvement in the global green economy, including exports of clean technology, renewable energy solutions, and critical minerals required for battery and renewable industries.

4. Environmental Considerations

The decline of fossil fuels in Canada aligns with the country's climate targets and presents new environmental opportunities:

- **Reduced Carbon Emissions:** The oil sands are one of Canada's largest sources of greenhouse gas emissions, so a reduction in oil production would significantly reduce the country's carbon footprint, aligning it closer to international climate commitments.

- **Environmental Restoration:** Areas impacted by oil sands extraction and pipeline construction could benefit from restoration efforts. With lower dependence on fossil fuels, Canada may have the capacity to focus on ecological rehabilitation in affected regions.

- **Investments in Renewable Energy:** Canada has extensive potential for renewable energy, particularly in hydropower, wind, and solar. Expanding renewable energy infrastructure can provide cleaner, reliable energy while supporting job creation in a sustainable economy.

5. Transition Strategies

Canada's transition from fossil fuels to renewable energy will require a combination of economic, policy, and social measures:

- **Federal and Provincial Coordination:** Effective collaboration between federal and provincial governments is essential to ensure that transition policies reflect regional needs, particularly for oil-producing provinces. This includes developing infrastructure, diversifying the economy, and creating job opportunities.

- **Retraining Programs and Employment Support:** Canada must prioritize reskilling and retraining workers in the fossil fuel industry to transition into emerging sectors like renewable energy, technology, and green construction. Targeted job support will be vital to ensure a just transition for affected communities.

- **Indigenous Partnerships in Clean Energy:** Engaging Indigenous communities as partners in clean energy projects will create opportunities for sustainable development and employment in these communities, while promoting environmental stewardship.
- **Policy Incentives for Clean Energy:** Policies such as tax credits, subsidies for clean technology, and incentives for renewable energy investments can accelerate Canada's transition to a low-carbon economy. Ensuring support for innovations in sectors like hydrogen and energy storage will also be important.

6. Conclusion

Canada faces both challenges and opportunities in the transition away from fossil fuels. While oil-dependent provinces will experience economic strain, Canada's abundant natural resources position it well to lead in renewable energy and clean technology. A successful transition will require collaboration between federal and provincial governments, investments in workforce development, and engagement with Indigenous communities. By advancing sustainable energy solutions and fostering regional resilience, Canada can emerge as a global leader in the green economy, promoting economic stability and environmental stewardship in the coming decades.

H. Middle East (Gulf Cooperation Council - GCC States)

The Gulf Cooperation Council (GCC) states—Saudi Arabia, United Arab Emirates, Kuwait, Qatar, Oman, and Bahrain—are some of the world's largest oil and gas producers, with economies largely dependent on fossil fuel exports. The global shift away from fossil fuels presents profound challenges and opportunities for these nations as they prepare for a post-oil future.

1. Economic Impact

The GCC economies are heavily reliant on oil and gas exports, making the decline of the fossil fuel industry a critical threat to their economic stability:

- **Revenue Reduction and Fiscal Challenges:** Oil and gas exports constitute a significant portion of government revenue in GCC states, with some countries deriving over 70% of their income from fossil fuels. A decline in demand and prices could lead to budget deficits, especially in countries like Oman and Bahrain, which have smaller financial reserves.
- **Diversification Pressure:** GCC countries have been working to diversify their economies, as seen in Saudi Arabia's Vision 2030 and the UAE's Vision 2021, which focus on sectors like tourism, technology, and finance. The rapid decline of fossil fuels may accelerate the need for economic diversification to maintain economic stability and employment.
- **Impact on Employment and Business:** Many jobs in the GCC are directly tied to the oil and gas industry, from extraction to refining and exports. With declining oil revenues, layoffs in the energy sector could rise, affecting both domestic and expatriate workers. Additionally, many businesses rely on government contracts and spending, which may decrease if revenues decline.

2. Social Impact

The transition away from fossil fuels will have broad social implications across the GCC states:

- **Impact on Living Standards and Public Services:** GCC citizens have benefited from high standards of living, supported by government subsidies and welfare programs funded by oil revenues. A decline in oil income could force governments to reduce subsidies on fuel, electricity, and water, as well as cut public spending on education, healthcare, and housing, potentially affecting quality of life.
- **Population Changes and Workforce Composition:** Many GCC economies are reliant on a large expatriate workforce. As opportunities in the oil sector shrink, there may be a shift in labor demand, potentially leading to a decrease in expatriate populations and a need to retrain nationals for employment in emerging sectors.
- **Youth Employment and Skills Development:** With a young population eager for employment opportunities, GCC states will face increasing pressure to provide meaningful, sustainable jobs outside the fossil fuel industry. Investment in education, skills training, and entrepreneurship will be essential to meet this demand.

3. Geopolitical Impact

The decline of fossil fuels will have substantial geopolitical implications for the GCC states, both regionally and globally:

- **Shifts in Regional Influence:** Fossil fuel resources have bolstered the GCC's regional influence and global alliances, particularly with energy-importing nations. As the world moves away from fossil fuels, the GCC's geopolitical leverage may diminish, potentially altering the balance of power in the Middle East and affecting relationships with energy-importing nations like the United States and China.

- **Increased Focus on Renewable Energy Diplomacy:** The GCC states have begun investing in renewable energy projects domestically and abroad, with a focus on solar and nuclear power. By positioning themselves as leaders in the energy transition, GCC countries could retain their influence in the global energy market and foster new alliances focused on sustainable energy.
- **Regional Cooperation on Sustainability Goals:** The GCC states may find renewed opportunities for cooperation on climate change and sustainability initiatives, both within the region and with neighboring countries. Shared renewable energy projects, particularly solar energy initiatives, could benefit multiple states while reducing carbon emissions.

4. Environmental Considerations

The shift away from fossil fuels presents GCC states with significant environmental challenges and opportunities:

- **Climate Change Mitigation Efforts:** As some of the world's largest per capita emitters of greenhouse gases, GCC states have faced pressure to reduce emissions. The decline of fossil fuels may encourage investments in carbon capture and renewable energy, helping them to meet climate commitments and reduce their environmental footprint.
- **Investment in Renewable Energy Projects:** GCC countries have vast potential for solar energy, and many have begun investing heavily in solar projects. Saudi Arabia and the UAE, for instance, have established ambitious targets for renewable energy capacity. Expanding these projects could reduce

dependence on oil and gas while providing sustainable power to meet growing domestic energy demand.

- **Water and Food Security:** The GCC's reliance on desalination, which is energy-intensive and traditionally powered by fossil fuels, is another concern. Renewable energy sources could power desalination plants more sustainably, addressing water scarcity while reducing greenhouse gas emissions. Investment in agricultural innovation will also be crucial to enhance food security in the region.

5. Transition Strategies

To address the decline in fossil fuel reliance, GCC states will need to implement comprehensive transition strategies:

- **Economic Diversification through Sovereign Wealth Funds:** GCC nations with substantial sovereign wealth funds, such as Saudi Arabia's Public Investment Fund (PIF) and the UAE's Mubadala, are investing in non-oil sectors domestically and abroad. These funds can provide a buffer against revenue loss while supporting long-term economic diversification efforts.

- **Investment in Human Capital:** Developing a workforce with skills in technology, finance, healthcare, and renewable energy is essential. GCC governments are investing in education and training programs, with a particular focus on STEM fields to prepare citizens for a post-oil economy.

- **Incentivizing Private Sector Growth:** The public sector has traditionally been the largest employer in the GCC. Policies that encourage private sector growth, innovation, and foreign direct investment in non-oil industries will create job opportunities and reduce dependence on government spending.

- **Renewable Energy as a Strategic Priority:** Expanding solar, wind, and nuclear energy infrastructure will be critical for meeting future energy needs sustainably. Countries like Saudi Arabia have announced large-scale renewable energy projects, such as the NEOM smart city, which emphasizes green technology.
- **Policies Supporting Sustainability and Green Technology:** By establishing policies to support green innovation, clean technology, and sustainable construction, the GCC can create new industries that support economic resilience while aligning with global sustainability trends.

6. Conclusion

The GCC states face unique challenges as global demand for fossil fuels declines. Given their heavy reliance on oil revenues, this transition will require bold economic diversification, investment in renewable energy, and sustainable policies to create resilient, diversified economies. By taking a proactive approach to economic transformation, the GCC states can secure a sustainable and prosperous future while continuing to play a role in the global energy landscape, albeit with a new emphasis on renewable energy and sustainable practices.

I. Indonesia

Indonesia, as Southeast Asia's largest economy and one of the world's largest coal exporters, is heavily reliant on fossil fuels for economic growth and energy generation. The global shift away from fossil fuels poses both challenges and opportunities for Indonesia as it seeks to meet climate commitments while sustaining economic growth and addressing social impacts.

1. Economic Impact

The decline of the fossil fuel industry could impact Indonesia's economy in several significant ways:

- **Loss of Coal Export Revenue:** Indonesia is one of the top coal exporters globally, with coal being a major revenue source, especially for regions like Kalimantan and Sumatra. As demand for coal declines, Indonesia's coal sector may face reduced earnings, impacting provincial revenues and leading to budgetary pressures, particularly in coal-dependent regions.
- **Investment Shift and Growth in Renewable Sectors:** The decline in fossil fuels may accelerate investment in renewables, such as geothermal, solar, and hydropower. Indonesia has vast geothermal potential as it sits on the Pacific Ring of Fire, which could become a primary focus as the nation transitions to cleaner energy sources.
- **Pressure on Employment:** Coal and oil industries employ significant numbers of workers in Indonesia. A reduction in these sectors could lead to job losses and impact households reliant on fossil fuel income, particularly in regions where alternative job opportunities are limited.

2. Social Impact

The shift away from fossil fuels will have a range of social implications across Indonesia:

- **Job Displacement in Coal Regions:** Communities in coal-rich regions like East Kalimantan may experience high job displacement. This will require substantial support in terms of job retraining, education, and economic diversification to prevent an increase in poverty and economic inequality.

- **Rural-Urban Disparities:** The transition to renewable energy may lead to a concentration of new opportunities in urban areas. Policymakers will need to address rural disparities by investing in green projects that generate rural employment and economic growth outside of traditional fossil fuel sectors.

- **Health and Environmental Benefits:** Moving away from coal could bring substantial public health benefits by reducing air pollution, which is a significant issue in many urban areas. Improved air quality could lead to lower healthcare costs and increased quality of life for millions of Indonesians.

3. Geopolitical Impact

Indonesia's geopolitical position as a major coal exporter may be impacted by the global transition to clean energy:

- **Shift in Trade Dynamics:** As countries like China, Japan, and South Korea—key markets for Indonesian coal—reduce coal imports in favor of renewable energy, Indonesia may need to diversify its export economy to maintain trade stability and ensure resilient economic partnerships.

- **Regional Leadership in Energy Transition:** Indonesia is a member of the G20 and has taken steps to enhance its role in regional climate initiatives. Leading in renewable energy and sustainable practices could enhance Indonesia's regional influence and attract green investments.

- **Energy Security Concerns:** As Indonesia transitions away from fossil fuels, the government must ensure that domestic energy production is sufficient to meet growing energy demand. Investing in domestic renewables can enhance energy security and reduce dependency on imported energy resources.

4. Environmental Considerations

The transition away from fossil fuels aligns with Indonesia's environmental goals and presents significant opportunities for conservation and sustainability:

- **Climate Change Mitigation Efforts:** Indonesia is one of the world's largest greenhouse gas emitters, largely due to deforestation, peatland degradation, and coal use. Shifting away from coal can contribute to Indonesia's climate targets and reduce emissions, which will be critical for achieving commitments under the Paris Agreement.
- **Preservation of Ecosystems and Forests:** The fossil fuel industry, particularly coal mining, has been linked to deforestation and environmental degradation. Reducing dependence on fossil fuels can provide opportunities to protect forests, which are vital for biodiversity and carbon sequestration.
- **Expansion of Renewable Energy Projects:** Indonesia has substantial renewable energy potential, especially in geothermal and solar power. Expanding these resources can help Indonesia meet domestic energy needs while reducing environmental impacts.

5. Transition Strategies

Indonesia's transition from fossil fuels to a low-carbon economy will require targeted strategies across various sectors:

- **Economic Diversification and Regional Development:** Policymakers must prioritize economic diversification in coal-producing regions by supporting alternative industries like ecotourism, agriculture, and manufacturing. This can help reduce regional disparities and mitigate the social impacts of coal's decline.

- **Investment in Clean Energy Infrastructure:** Developing renewable energy infrastructure, particularly in geothermal and solar power, can enhance energy security and provide sustainable employment. Encouraging private sector investment through incentives and partnerships will be crucial to achieving renewable energy targets.
- **Retraining Programs and Social Support:** Indonesia will need to invest in retraining programs for workers in the coal and oil industries to help them transition to new roles in renewables, technology, and green construction. Providing social safety nets for impacted communities will also be essential to a fair transition.
- **Policies and Incentives for Green Growth:** Incentives for renewable energy projects, coupled with policies to phase out coal, can accelerate Indonesia's transition. Policies aimed at reducing emissions, promoting energy efficiency, and supporting green technology will also align with global sustainability trends.
- **Community Engagement and Transparency:** Engaging local communities in the transition planning process will help build public support and ensure equitable outcomes. Transparency around government plans, timelines, and support mechanisms will be crucial to minimize social disruptions.

6. Conclusion

Indonesia's reliance on fossil fuels, particularly coal, presents significant challenges as global demand declines. However, with abundant renewable energy resources, Indonesia has an opportunity to become a regional leader in clean energy. By prioritizing economic diversification, investing in renewables, and supporting social programs for impacted workers, Indonesia can secure a more sustainable and resilient economic future. With concerted efforts, the country can contribute to global climate goals while improving the quality of life for its citizens and protecting its rich natural environment.

5. Global Timeline of the Transition

- **2020s:** Early impacts on coal-producing regions, reduced investment in new oil and gas projects, increasing adoption of electric vehicles, and renewable energy infrastructure.
- **2030s:** Significant reduction in oil demand, major economic restructuring in fossil fuel-dependent countries, full-scale electrification of transportation, and stabilization of renewable energy dominance in electricity generation.
- **2040s:** Oil and coal sectors significantly reduced globally, with fossil fuel use mostly confined to niche applications. Major fossil fuel producers experience deep economic and geopolitical shifts.

6. Opportunities for Countries

Countries less reliant on fossil fuels, or those that proactively diversify their economies, will benefit from the transition. Investments in renewable energy technologies, electric mobility, and sustainable infrastructure will create new industries and job opportunities.

A. Renewable Energy Pioneers (Germany, China, Denmark)

- These countries have already positioned themselves as leaders in renewable energy. Their early investments are likely to pay off in terms of global leadership in the green economy.

B. Developing Economies (India, Brazil)

- As fossil fuel costs rise and renewable energy becomes cheaper, developing nations like India and Brazil may leapfrog traditional energy infrastructure, benefiting from decentralized energy sources like solar and wind.

7. Conclusion

The decline of the fossil fuel industry will have profound impacts across the globe, with oil-dependent nations facing the most severe consequences. While some countries will struggle with economic and social disruptions, others will seize the opportunity to lead in the global energy transition. The timeline for these changes spans the next two to three decades, with fossil fuel industries entering a sustained period of contraction by the 2030s. Countries must prepare for this shift by investing in renewable energy, diversifying their economies, and creating robust safety nets for workers in fossil fuel industries.

Global Timeline of the Transition Away from Fossil Fuels

The transition away from fossil fuels is a gradual process influenced by political, technological, economic, and social factors, with varying impacts across countries. Here is a general timeline that outlines the expected phases of transition over the coming decades:

2020s: Foundations and Early Transition

- **Policy Commitments and Goals:** Many countries have set ambitious targets to reduce emissions and shift toward renewables. Key agreements, such as the Paris Climate Agreement, push countries to set policies to reach net-zero emissions by 2050 or sooner.

- **Investment in Renewable Energy:** Global investments in solar, wind, and battery technologies grow, supported by falling costs and improved efficiency. Renewable energy starts to outcompete coal and natural gas in certain regions.

- **Coal Phase-Out Initiatives:** Countries like Germany, Canada, and the UK lead in phasing out coal, with other developed economies setting target dates to reduce or eliminate coal power.
- **Increased Focus on Electric Vehicles (EVs):** The EV market accelerates, with major automakers committing to phasing out internal combustion engines (ICEs). Governments, including those in Europe and China, introduce bans on new ICE vehicle sales starting as early as 2030.
- **Development of Green Finance:** Green bonds, carbon trading, and sustainability-linked finance become increasingly popular, supporting projects in renewable energy and clean technology.

2030s: Acceleration and Scaling

- **Broad Electrification of Energy Systems:** Rapid growth in renewable energy production, combined with energy storage advancements, leads to more electricity generation from clean sources. Many countries see renewables surpass fossil fuels as the dominant energy source.
- **Major Reductions in Oil Demand for Transport:** The EV market matures, with electric cars and public transportation becoming mainstream. Oil demand declines significantly in the transportation sector, impacting oil-dependent countries.
- **Emergence of New Energy Technologies:** Breakthroughs in green hydrogen, carbon capture, utilization, and storage (CCUS), and advanced nuclear reactors become viable on a

larger scale, aiding decarbonization in hard-to-electrify sectors like heavy industry and long-haul transport.

- **Economic Diversification in Oil-Dependent Economies:** Oil-dependent countries, especially in the Middle East, have accelerated their economic diversification strategies. The success of these initiatives varies, with countries focused on tourism, technology, and finance experiencing more stability.
- **Coal Almost Phased Out in Developed Countries:** Coal power plants become scarce in high-income nations, replaced by renewables, storage, and nuclear. Developing countries also move to reduce coal reliance with international financial support.
- **Public Support for Climate Action:** Societal awareness and demand for climate action grow as more communities experience climate-related disasters. Policy support for renewables and green infrastructure increases globally.

2040s: Maturity and Systemic Transition

- **Energy Systems Dominated by Renewables:** Renewables, particularly solar, wind, hydro, and geothermal, account for most of the global electricity supply. Energy storage systems become efficient and widespread, making renewable energy reliable 24/7.
- **Oil Use Limited to Specialty Sectors:** Oil demand is reduced to specialty applications in petrochemicals and aviation, where alternative fuels and biofuels make up the majority of fuel needs. Global oil production is a fraction of its peak.
- **Global Hydrogen Economy Growth:** Hydrogen becomes a mainstream energy carrier, especially in sectors like shipping, aviation, and heavy industries. Hydrogen infrastructure

expands, supported by clean hydrogen production methods, such as electrolysis using renewable energy.

- **Net-Zero Achievements in Leading Countries:** Some countries and regions achieve net-zero emissions, having successfully transitioned their power, transportation, and industrial sectors to low-carbon alternatives. Remaining emissions are offset with carbon removal technologies.
- **Fossil Fuel Phased Out for Heating and Industrial Uses:** Alternatives to natural gas for heating and industrial use become mainstream, with solutions like electric heat pumps and industrial electrification achieving widespread adoption.
- **Increased Focus on Carbon Sequestration and Climate Resilience:** Carbon capture and storage, along with natural carbon sinks (like reforestation and soil carbon projects), play a larger role in offsetting remaining emissions. Countries focus on climate adaptation infrastructure to manage climate risks.

2050s: Stabilization and Long-Term Sustainability

- **Global Achievement of Net-Zero Targets:** Most developed countries, and many developing ones, achieve net-zero emissions or near-zero emissions status, having transitioned fully from fossil fuels to renewable energy and green technologies.
- **Fossil Fuel Economy Reduced to Minimal Applications:** Fossil fuel use is largely confined to specific industrial needs where alternatives are either impractical or expensive. Oil and gas companies either diversify into renewables or focus on specialty applications and carbon sequestration.

- **Universal Electrification and Access to Clean Energy:** Electrification extends globally, with clean, reliable, and affordable energy available to nearly all. Renewables provide the majority of energy needs worldwide, with decentralized power solutions supporting remote and rural communities.
- **Global Collaboration on Climate Solutions:** Continued collaboration on climate action remains essential, focusing on maintaining sustainable practices, advancing carbon-negative technologies, and enhancing biodiversity and ecosystem restoration.
- **Monitoring and Maintenance of Sustainable Systems:** Transitioned energy and industrial systems are now monitored for sustainability, efficiency, and resilience. Maintenance of carbon-neutral infrastructure becomes standard practice globally.

Summary

2020s: The foundation is laid for energy transition through policy commitments, initial renewables growth, and early phase-outs of fossil fuels.

2030s: Transition accelerates, with renewables taking a more central role in energy systems, EVs becoming mainstream, and new technologies emerging.

2040s: Renewables dominate, fossil fuel use is largely reduced to specific applications, and many countries achieve net-zero emissions.

2050s: Global energy systems stabilize around renewables, nearly all countries reach net-zero or near-zero emissions, and fossil fuel use is minimal, signaling a fully transitioned global economy.

This timeline will vary by country and region, with economic, political, and social factors influencing the pace and effectiveness of each transition.

Chapter Four
Cost of global warming in the next 25 years

There are two sides to the cost associated with global warming. The one side involves the economic cost of global warming that will result from property destruction, infrastructure destruction, crop failures, and the relocation of millions of people from low lying areas to higher ground. The other side is the cost that will occur resulting from lost revenue and the decline in physical assets such as exploration equipment, refineries, distribution networks, and proven reserves which will never be used.

Projecting the cost on both sides of this equation will depend upon how rapidly the planet transitions from fossil fuels to renewable energy. The quicker the transition to renewable energy the lesser impact on the global environment. On the other hand, the quicker the transition away from fossil fuels the quicker the economic impact on the Fossil fuel industry. Thus, the numbers on either side of the equation are not absolute numbers even if they could be calculated in the first place But rather estimates made by people focusing on one side or the other.

Estimates of the negative economic impact of global warming over the next 25 years range from $20 trillion to $40 trillion. Though the exact breakdown would depend on the source of the estimate, component costs typically stem from various factors, including:

Agricultural Losses

Agricultural losses due to climate change represent a significant component of the overall cost of global warming, affecting food production, food prices, and economic stability, particularly in regions dependent on agriculture. These losses stem from several climate-related factors that negatively impact crop yields, livestock, and fisheries. Here's a detailed breakdown of how climate change will drive agricultural losses:

1. Crop Yield Reductions

- **Heat Stress**: Higher temperatures can reduce crop yields by stressing plants and shortening their growing seasons. Staple crops like wheat, maize, and rice are particularly sensitive to temperature increases, especially during key growth stages like pollination.
- **Droughts**: Prolonged droughts will limit water availability for irrigation and natural rainfall-dependent agriculture, leading to significant yield reductions in crops. Regions like Sub-Saharan Africa, South Asia, and parts of the U.S. will be particularly vulnerable.
- **Changing Growing Seasons**: Shifts in growing seasons and the timing of rainfall patterns can disrupt traditional planting and harvesting cycles, leading to lower productivity and harvest failures.
- **Soil Degradation**: Increased temperatures and irregular rainfall patterns can cause soil erosion, degradation, and nutrient loss, further reducing crop productivity.

2. Increased Pest and Disease Pressure

- **Expanding Pest Ranges**: Warmer temperatures allow pests and insects (like locusts, aphids, and beetles) to expand their range and thrive in regions where they were previously limited by cooler climates. This will increase crop losses due to pest damage.

- **Crop Diseases**: Higher humidity and warmer temperatures favor the spread of crop diseases like fungal infections, blights, and molds, which can devastate yields. For example, the spread of wheat rust and rice blast disease is expected to worsen with climate change.

3. Water Scarcity and Irrigation Challenges

- **Reduced Water Availability**: Droughts and changing precipitation patterns will reduce water availability for irrigation in key agricultural regions. Areas dependent on rivers fed by glacial melt (e.g., parts of India, China, and South America) will experience significant water shortages as glaciers retreat.
- **Increased Irrigation Costs**: Farmers will need to invest in more advanced irrigation systems and water management practices to cope with less reliable water supplies. The cost of these adaptations, along with the energy needed to pump and distribute water, will add to agricultural expenses.

4. Livestock and Animal Agriculture Losses

- **Heat Stress on Livestock**: Higher temperatures can reduce livestock productivity by causing heat stress, which lowers milk production, reproductive rates, and growth in cattle, poultry, and other livestock. This can also lead to higher mortality rates during heatwaves.
- **Water and Feed Shortages**: Water scarcity, along with drought-related crop failures, will lead to feed shortages,

raising the cost of maintaining livestock. This will drive up meat and dairy prices.

- **Disease Spread**: Warmer and wetter conditions can expand the range of diseases that affect livestock, such as tick-borne diseases and parasitic infections, leading to higher mortality and veterinary costs.

5. Fisheries and Aquaculture Losses

- **Ocean Warming and Acidification**: Rising ocean temperatures and acidification (due to increased CO2 absorption) will damage marine ecosystems, including coral reefs and fish stocks. Key species like tuna, cod, and shellfish are expected to decline in abundance, affecting both wild fisheries and aquaculture.
- **Shifting Fish Populations**: Fish populations are moving toward cooler waters, disrupting traditional fishing grounds and making it harder for coastal communities to sustain their livelihoods.
- **Reduced Fish Reproduction**: Ocean acidification affects the reproductive health of fish species and shellfish, reducing their ability to reproduce and grow. This threatens the sustainability of marine food sources.

6. Impact on Global Food Security

- **Food Price Increases**: Reduced agricultural output will drive up food prices, disproportionately affecting low-income populations. This will increase hunger, malnutrition, and food insecurity, particularly in vulnerable regions like Africa and South Asia.
- **Disruption of Food Supply Chains**: Climate change will disrupt food supply chains due to extreme weather events,

transport failures, and trade restrictions. This can lead to localized food shortages and inflation.

- **Shifts in Global Agricultural Productivity**: While some regions (like Northern Europe and parts of Canada) may see temporary gains in crop yields due to warmer temperatures, most tropical and subtropical regions will experience significant declines, exacerbating global inequalities in food production.

7. Adaptation Costs

- **Investment in Resilient Crop Varieties**: To cope with changing climate conditions, farmers will need to adopt more resilient crop varieties that can withstand heat, drought, and pests. Developing and deploying these crops will require significant investment in research, seed distribution, and farming practices.
- **New Agricultural Practices**: Farmers will need to invest in climate-smart agriculture practices, including precision farming, soil management, and water conservation techniques. These adaptations will come at a cost, particularly for smallholder farmers in developing countries.
- **Technological Upgrades**: To mitigate the impact of climate change, many farms will need to adopt new technologies, such as advanced irrigation systems, sensors, and climate modeling tools, to optimize water use and protect crops. These costs could be prohibitive for many farmers, especially in poorer regions.

8. Economic and Social Impacts

- **Loss of Rural Livelihoods**: Agriculture is a primary livelihood for millions of people worldwide, especially in developing countries. Climate-induced agricultural losses will lead to reduced incomes for farmers, rural poverty, and increased migration to urban areas.

- **Loss of Agricultural Exports**: Countries that rely heavily on agricultural exports (e.g., Brazil, Argentina, and parts of Africa and Asia) will suffer economically as reduced crop yields lower export volumes, affecting trade balances and national economies.

Regional Impact of Agricultural Losses

The impact of climate change on agriculture will vary by region:

- **Tropical and Subtropical Regions**: These areas, which include much of Africa, Southeast Asia, and parts of Latin America, will see the greatest agricultural losses due to increased heat, droughts, and changing rainfall patterns.
- **Mid-Latitude Regions**: Parts of North America, Europe, and Asia will also face significant losses, especially in regions that rely heavily on irrigation or are prone to droughts and extreme weather.
- **Polar and Northern Regions**: Some northern regions may initially benefit from longer growing seasons, but this will be offset by other climate-related risks, such as increased pest pressure and changing precipitation patterns.

Economic Examples of Agricultural Losses

- **2010 Russian Heatwave**: The extreme heatwave reduced Russia's wheat harvest by 30%, leading to global food price spikes.

- **2018 European Drought**: Severe drought across Europe reduced crop yields by up to 50% in some areas, affecting wheat, corn, and potato production.
- **2020-2021 U.S. Drought**: The prolonged drought in the western U.S. caused widespread crop failures and led to water restrictions for farmers, reducing output in key agricultural regions like California's Central Valley.

Summary

Agricultural losses from climate change will be driven by a complex mix of factors, including heat stress, water scarcity, increased pests and diseases, and disruptions to fisheries. The resulting economic costs will be felt globally, particularly in regions where agriculture is a major component of the economy. These losses will also have severe implications for food security, livelihoods, and social stability, necessitating urgent adaptation efforts to mitigate the damage.

Health Costs

Health costs related to climate change are another significant component of the overall economic burden, as global warming directly and indirectly affects human health through heat stress, disease spread, air quality deterioration, and malnutrition. These impacts will strain healthcare systems, increase mortality and morbidity, and drive up healthcare expenditures worldwide. Below is a detailed breakdown of the health-related costs of climate change:

1. Heat-related Illnesses and Deaths

- **Heat Stress and Heatwaves**: As global temperatures rise, more people will be exposed to dangerous levels of heat. Heatwaves can cause heatstroke, dehydration, cardiovascular problems, and other heat-related illnesses, particularly affecting vulnerable populations like the elderly, children, and those with preexisting health conditions.

  - **Healthcare Costs**: Increased hospital admissions, emergency services, and treatments related to heat-related illnesses will drive up healthcare expenditures.
  - **Mortality Costs**: Higher mortality rates during heatwaves will lead to economic losses in terms of lost productivity, human capital, and the burden on healthcare systems. The **2019 European heatwave**, for example, caused over 1,500 deaths in France alone.

2. Spread of Infectious Diseases

- **Vector-borne Diseases**: Warmer temperatures and changing precipitation patterns will expand the range of mosquitoes and other vectors that transmit diseases like **malaria, dengue fever, Zika virus,** and **Lyme disease**. Regions that were previously less affected by these diseases will become more vulnerable, increasing infection rates.
  - **Treatment Costs**: The spread of these diseases will raise healthcare costs for diagnosis, treatment, and prevention efforts like vaccination campaigns and mosquito control.
  - **Lost Productivity**: Individuals who contract these diseases may face long periods of illness or disability, leading to lost productivity and additional economic strain on families and communities.
- **Water-borne Diseases**: Increased flooding and heavy rainfall can lead to the contamination of drinking water, increasing the spread of water-borne diseases like **cholera, typhoid**, and

diarrheal diseases. These are particularly deadly for children in developing countries.

3. Respiratory and Cardiovascular Diseases

- **Air Quality Degradation**: Climate change worsens air pollution, as higher temperatures increase the formation of ground-level **ozone** and exacerbate **wildfires**. Poor air quality is linked to respiratory diseases like **asthma, chronic obstructive pulmonary disease (COPD),** and lung cancer, as well as cardiovascular problems like heart attacks and strokes.
    - **Medical Costs**: More frequent hospitalizations, medications, and treatments for chronic respiratory and cardiovascular conditions will significantly increase healthcare costs. The **wildfire season in California** in 2020, for example, led to a spike in emergency room visits due to respiratory issues.
    - **Premature Deaths**: Long-term exposure to air pollution will increase premature deaths, which come with an economic cost in terms of lost productivity and the financial burden on families and healthcare systems.

4. Mental Health Impacts

- **Climate Anxiety**: The growing awareness of climate change and its potential impacts can lead to anxiety, depression, and stress, particularly among younger generations. This phenomenon, often referred to as "eco-anxiety" or "climate anxiety," is becoming more prevalent.
- **Trauma from Disasters**: People who experience natural disasters (like hurricanes, floods, and wildfires) are at increased risk for **post-traumatic stress disorder (PTSD),**

depression, and other mental health issues. The psychological impact of displacement, loss of homes, and economic hardship can be profound.

- **Mental Health Services**: The increased need for mental health services (therapy, counseling, medications) will place additional demands on healthcare systems.

5. Food Security and Malnutrition

- **Crop Failures and Food Shortages**: As agricultural yields decline due to climate change, food prices will rise, making it harder for vulnerable populations to access sufficient nutrition. This can lead to **malnutrition**, particularly in developing countries, which increases susceptibility to infectious diseases and impairs cognitive development in children.
    - **Healthcare Costs**: Treating malnutrition and related health issues will increase healthcare expenditures, particularly in regions where healthcare systems are already under strain.
    - **Developmental Impacts**: Malnutrition in early childhood has long-term impacts on cognitive development and productivity, which will result in reduced human capital and economic productivity in the long run.

6. Water-related Health Risks

- **Increased Flooding and Water Contamination**: More frequent floods and storms will increase the risk of water contamination, leading to the spread of diseases like **diarrhea, cholera,** and **hepatitis A**. Poor sanitation and access to clean water, especially in developing regions, will exacerbate these risks.

 - **Sanitation and Healthcare Costs**: Countries will need to invest more in water sanitation infrastructure and healthcare treatments to cope with the increased burden of waterborne diseases.

7. Occupational Health Risks

- **Outdoor Workers**: Workers in agriculture, construction, and other outdoor industries are particularly vulnerable to heat stress. Longer and more intense heatwaves will reduce labor productivity, as workers take more frequent breaks or fall ill.
  - **Productivity Losses**: Heat-induced productivity losses can affect economic output, particularly in sectors dependent on manual labor.
  - **Increased Healthcare Expenditures**: More hospital visits and healthcare needs for workers affected by extreme heat will place additional pressure on healthcare systems.

8. Vulnerable Populations

- **Elderly and Low-Income Communities**: Older adults are particularly susceptible to heat-related illnesses and the effects of poor air quality. Low-income communities, especially those with inadequate housing, are also more vulnerable to climate impacts, as they often lack the resources to adapt or access healthcare.
  - **Social and Healthcare Costs**: These vulnerable populations will require more medical attention, driving up healthcare costs and placing further strain on social services.

9. Costs of Adaptation in the Healthcare Sector

- **Health Infrastructure Investment**: To cope with the growing health impacts of climate change, countries will need to invest in more resilient healthcare infrastructure, including cooling systems in hospitals, improved disease surveillance systems, and expanded emergency services.
- **Public Health Campaigns**: Governments will need to invest in public health campaigns to raise awareness about heat-related illnesses, vector-borne diseases, and mental health impacts, which will require significant financial resources.

Regional Health Costs from Climate Change

The health impacts of climate change will vary by region:

- **Tropical and Subtropical Regions**: These regions will see the greatest increase in vector-borne diseases, malnutrition, and heat-related illnesses due to rising temperatures and changes in rainfall patterns.
- **Developed Countries**: While developed countries may have more resilient healthcare systems, they will still face rising costs due to increased heat-related illnesses, respiratory issues from wildfires, and mental health challenges.
- **Developing Countries**: Developing countries, particularly in Africa and South Asia, will bear the brunt of health costs due to weaker healthcare systems, higher exposure to climate risks, and larger vulnerable populations.

Economic Examples of Health Costs

- **Europe's 2003 Heatwave**: This event resulted in an estimated 70,000 excess deaths and cost billions in health-related expenditures across Europe.

- **U.S. Wildfires (2020)**: Wildfires across the western U.S. led to a significant increase in hospital admissions for respiratory and cardiovascular issues, with health costs estimated in the hundreds of millions.

Summary

Health costs driven by climate change will be substantial and multifaceted. These costs will arise from increased heat-related illnesses and deaths, the spread of infectious diseases, poor air quality, food insecurity, water contamination, and mental health issues. As global temperatures rise, these health impacts will place increasing pressure on healthcare systems, particularly in regions with less adaptive capacity, contributing to the overall economic burden of climate change.

Economic Disruptions

Economic disruptions due to climate change will arise from the broad range of impacts that affect industries, labor productivity, trade, supply chains, and overall economic stability. These disruptions can reduce global economic output, increase volatility in financial markets, and exacerbate inequality between countries and regions. Below is an analysis of the specific ways climate change will disrupt economies worldwide:

1. Disruptions to Global Supply Chains

- **Extreme Weather Events**: Hurricanes, floods, wildfires, and storms will increasingly damage infrastructure critical to supply chains, such as ports, roads, railways, and airports. This will delay shipments of goods, disrupt manufacturing processes, and increase costs for businesses.
    - **Example**: Hurricane Harvey (2017) disrupted oil production and refining in the Gulf Coast, leading to a

surge in gasoline prices and delays in industrial production across the U.S.

- **Logistical Bottlenecks**: Climate-related disruptions can lead to bottlenecks in global supply chains, affecting industries such as agriculture, electronics, automotive, and pharmaceuticals. Delays in the delivery of raw materials, intermediate goods, or finished products will increase costs and reduce profits.

- **Impact on Global Trade**: Regions like Southeast Asia, which are integral to global manufacturing and trade, are highly vulnerable to climate risks. Disruptions in these regions will have ripple effects on global trade, causing economic losses in countries that rely on imported goods or export-driven economies.

2. Reduced Agricultural Productivity

- **Food Price Volatility**: As climate change reduces agricultural productivity due to droughts, floods, and extreme weather, food prices will become more volatile. This will particularly impact low-income households, which spend a higher proportion of their income on food, leading to reduced consumer spending in other areas.

- **Global Trade of Agricultural Commodities**: Countries that rely on agricultural exports, such as Brazil (soybeans), the U.S. (corn and wheat), and Sub-Saharan Africa (coffee and cocoa), will experience economic losses as crop yields decline and global food markets become more unstable. This will increase trade imbalances and lead to disruptions in the global food supply.

- **Famine and Economic Instability**: In developing regions, especially those reliant on subsistence farming, climate-induced agricultural failures could lead to food shortages, triggering social unrest, migration, and economic instability.

3. Labor Productivity Losses

- **Heat Stress on Workers**: Rising temperatures and more frequent heatwaves will reduce labor productivity, especially in sectors that rely heavily on outdoor or manual labor, such as construction, agriculture, and mining. Workers in these sectors will face more frequent heat-related illnesses, reduced working hours, and lower efficiency.
    - **Economic Impact**: A 2019 study estimated that by 2030, heat stress could reduce global GDP by as much as $2.4 trillion due to lost labor productivity, particularly in tropical and subtropical regions like Southeast Asia, Sub-Saharan Africa, and parts of the U.S.
- **Indoor Work Environments**: Higher temperatures also affect productivity in indoor workplaces by increasing energy costs for cooling, reducing worker comfort, and leading to fatigue, especially in industries like manufacturing and services.

4. Damage to Critical Infrastructure

- **Costly Repairs and Replacements**: Climate change will increase the need for repairs, retrofits, and replacements of critical infrastructure such as roads, bridges, water treatment plants, and power grids. This will impose substantial costs on governments and businesses, diverting funds from other productive investments.
    - **Example**: In the U.S., the costs of maintaining and upgrading infrastructure to withstand climate impacts

are projected to be in the tens of billions of dollars annually by mid-century.

- **Disruption of Energy Systems**: Rising temperatures will put pressure on energy grids, increasing the likelihood of blackouts during heatwaves when demand spikes due to air conditioning. Additionally, extreme weather events can damage power generation and transmission infrastructure, disrupting electricity supply for businesses and homes.

5. Migration and Displacement

- **Climate Refugees**: As sea levels rise and extreme weather events increase, millions of people will be displaced from their homes, particularly in low-lying coastal areas and regions prone to drought and floods. The **World Bank** estimates that by 2050, more than 140 million people in Sub-Saharan Africa, South Asia, and Latin America could become climate migrants.
    - **Economic Consequences**: Large-scale migration can disrupt labor markets, strain social services, and increase competition for jobs and resources in receiving regions. In countries where internal or cross-border migration spikes, this can destabilize local economies and lead to political and social tensions.
- **Impact on Agriculture and Rural Economies**: Climate-induced migration from rural areas, where agricultural productivity declines, will exacerbate the labor shortages and economic collapse of these regions, further weakening food production and the local economy.

6. Strain on Financial Markets and Insurance

- **Increased Insurance Costs**: As climate risks become more severe and frequent, insurers will face rising costs from payouts related to extreme weather events, property damage, and health impacts. This will lead to higher insurance premiums for businesses and homeowners or, in some cases, the withdrawal of coverage in high-risk areas.
    - **Example**: In regions like Florida and California, rising insurance premiums due to climate risks are making property insurance increasingly unaffordable, leading to housing market instability.
- **Market Volatility**: Climate change will increase market volatility as sectors like agriculture, energy, and insurance experience higher costs and reduced profits. Financial markets will also be affected by uncertainty surrounding the future impacts of climate change on global economic growth.
- **Asset Devaluation**: Properties and investments in climate-vulnerable regions may lose value as risks from sea-level rise, wildfires, or hurricanes become more apparent. This could trigger economic downturns in regions heavily reliant on real estate and tourism.

7. Impact on Key Economic Sectors

- **Tourism**: Climate change will affect tourism in multiple ways. Rising temperatures, more frequent natural disasters, and ecosystem degradation (e.g., coral reef loss, forest fires) will reduce the appeal of certain tourist destinations, leading to a decline in revenue for regions that depend on tourism.
    - **Example**: Caribbean islands, which rely heavily on tourism, will suffer from more frequent hurricanes,

beach erosion, and the destruction of natural attractions like coral reefs.

- **Energy Sector**: The energy sector will face disruptions from both increased demand for cooling and damage to energy infrastructure from extreme weather events. Additionally, fossil fuel-dependent industries may experience financial losses as governments implement carbon pricing and transition to renewable energy sources.
- **Manufacturing and Industry**: Factories and industrial operations that rely on a stable climate and consistent access to raw materials, water, and energy will face production slowdowns and higher operating costs due to climate disruptions.

8. Government and Fiscal Pressures

- **Increased Government Spending**: Governments will need to increase spending on disaster relief, infrastructure repair, healthcare, and social services to address the impacts of climate change. This will place pressure on public finances, particularly in developing countries with limited resources.
- **Reduced Tax Revenues**: As climate change disrupts economic activity, governments may see a reduction in tax revenues from sectors like agriculture, tourism, and real estate. Lower productivity and higher unemployment rates due to climate disruptions will further strain public budgets.
- **Debt Burden**: Some countries may need to take on more debt to cope with the economic impacts of climate change, potentially leading to higher interest payments and reduced fiscal space for other priorities, such as education and infrastructure development.

9. Social Unrest and Political Instability

- **Economic Inequality**: The economic disruptions caused by climate change are likely to exacerbate inequalities, as poorer regions and populations bear the brunt of the impacts. Food shortages, water scarcity, and loss of livelihoods could lead to social unrest, protests, and conflicts, particularly in regions already facing political instability.
- **Economic Migration**: As climate impacts worsen, migration patterns could trigger tensions between countries or regions, particularly if climate refugees move into areas that are already economically stressed. This could lead to political instability, increased border conflicts, and economic isolation.

10. Cost of Adaptation and Mitigation

- **Investment in Adaptation**: To mitigate economic disruptions, governments and businesses will need to invest in climate-resilient infrastructure, new agricultural technologies, and improved water management systems. The cost of these investments will be significant, diverting resources from other areas of the economy.
- **Transition to Green Economies**: The global shift to renewable energy and sustainable practices will require substantial upfront investments in new technologies, retraining workers, and developing new industries. While this transition is essential for reducing the long-term impacts of climate change, it could create short-term economic disruptions as traditional industries decline.

Summary

Economic disruptions caused by climate change will be widespread, affecting global supply chains, labor productivity, agricultural output, financial markets, and infrastructure. These disruptions will exacerbate inequality, strain public finances, and increase the cost of doing business. In the long term, the economic toll of climate change could reduce global GDP growth and create instability in vulnerable regions, making adaptation and mitigation efforts essential to limit the damage.

Loss of biodiversity and ecosystem services

Loss of biodiversity and ecosystem services due to climate change is another significant component of the economic burden. Ecosystems provide critical services that support human well-being, from pollinating crops and purifying water to regulating the climate and providing materials for food, medicine, and industry. As biodiversity declines and ecosystems degrade, the loss of these services will have substantial economic consequences. Below is a breakdown of how biodiversity loss and ecosystem degradation will impact economies:

1. Loss of Ecosystem Services

- **Pollination**: Many crops, including fruits, vegetables, and nuts, rely on pollination by insects like bees, butterflies, and birds. Climate change, along with habitat destruction and pesticide use, threatens pollinator populations. The loss of pollinators will reduce agricultural yields, increasing food prices and impacting farmers' livelihoods.
    - **Economic Impact**: Pollination services are estimated to contribute over **$235–$577 billion** annually to global food production. The decline of pollinators would result in significant economic losses for the

agricultural sector, particularly in regions reliant on high-value crops like almonds and coffee.

- **Water Purification**: Wetlands, forests, and other ecosystems play a crucial role in filtering pollutants and maintaining clean water supplies. As these ecosystems degrade, water purification will become more expensive and less effective, leading to higher costs for water treatment and greater risks of waterborne diseases.
    - **Example**: The destruction of mangroves and wetlands, which naturally filter water and protect coastlines, can increase the cost of flood protection and water treatment in coastal communities.
- **Carbon Sequestration**: Forests, grasslands, and oceans absorb carbon dioxide from the atmosphere, mitigating climate change by acting as carbon sinks. The destruction of these ecosystems (e.g., deforestation, coral reef die-offs) reduces the Earth's capacity to sequester carbon, accelerating climate change and increasing the costs of adaptation and mitigation.
    - **Economic Impact**: The **global economic value of forests** for carbon sequestration alone is estimated at around **$200 billion** per year. The loss of these services will increase the costs of carbon mitigation strategies.
- **Soil Fertility and Erosion Control**: Healthy ecosystems maintain soil fertility and prevent erosion. As ecosystems degrade, soil quality declines, reducing agricultural productivity and increasing the risk of desertification, especially in arid regions. This will have severe economic impacts on farmers and agricultural communities.

  - **Example**: The loss of soil fertility due to land degradation could result in up to a **12% decline in crop yields** globally by 2050, with economic losses in the hundreds of billions of dollars annually.

2. Loss of Fisheries and Marine Resources

- **Decline of Fish Stocks**: Climate change is causing ocean temperatures to rise, altering marine ecosystems and leading to the collapse of fish populations. Overfishing and ocean acidification further exacerbate this trend. Coastal communities that depend on fisheries for their livelihoods will be particularly vulnerable to these changes.
  - **Economic Impact**: The global fishing industry is valued at around **$401 billion**, and over **3 billion people** rely on seafood as their primary source of protein. The decline of fish stocks will result in lost income, higher food prices, and unemployment in fishing communities.
- **Coral Reef Degradation**: Coral reefs provide essential services by protecting coastlines from erosion, supporting fisheries, and driving tourism. Warming oceans and ocean acidification are causing coral bleaching and mass die-offs of coral reefs, which will reduce biodiversity and harm marine ecosystems.
  - **Tourism Losses**: Coral reef-related tourism generates around **$36 billion** annually. The degradation of these ecosystems will result in lost revenue for regions like the Caribbean and Southeast Asia, which rely heavily on ecotourism.
  - **Fisheries Decline**: Coral reefs support more than **25% of marine species**, many of which are commercially

valuable. The loss of these ecosystems will negatively impact global fisheries and coastal economies.

3. Loss of Forests and Terrestrial Biodiversity

- **Deforestation and Habitat Loss**: Deforestation, particularly in tropical rainforests like the Amazon, threatens biodiversity by destroying habitats for countless species. These ecosystems provide crucial services such as regulating the climate, supporting the water cycle, and producing oxygen.
    - **Economic Impact**: Forest ecosystems contribute to industries such as timber, paper, and pharmaceuticals, generating billions of dollars annually. For example, the Amazon rainforest is responsible for producing a large portion of the world's oxygen and is critical for regulating global rainfall patterns, which directly impact agriculture.
- **Extinction of Medicinal Plants and Species**: Many pharmaceutical products are derived from plants and animals found in biodiverse ecosystems. The loss of species due to climate change could mean the loss of potential medicines and cures for diseases, as well as the economic value associated with these discoveries.
    - **Economic Value**: The **global pharmaceutical industry** relies heavily on natural products, with about **$60 billion** of the sector's annual revenue coming from medicines derived from biological sources.

4. Loss of Coastal Ecosystems

- **Mangroves, Seagrasses, and Wetlands**: Coastal ecosystems like mangroves, seagrasses, and wetlands provide critical services such as flood control, storm protection, and carbon sequestration. These ecosystems are threatened by rising sea levels, coastal development, and pollution.

- **Flood Protection**: Mangroves and wetlands can reduce the impact of storm surges by absorbing floodwaters. The loss of these ecosystems will increase the cost of artificial flood defenses, such as sea walls and levees.
- **Economic Impact**: Coastal protection services provided by mangroves alone are valued at **$82 billion** annually. The loss of these services will result in higher disaster recovery costs and greater economic losses for coastal communities.

- **Tourism and Recreation**: Coastal ecosystems attract millions of tourists each year, generating revenue for local economies. The degradation of these ecosystems will lead to a decline in ecotourism and recreational activities, negatively impacting businesses that rely on tourism.
    - **Example**: Florida's tourism industry, which generates around **$90 billion** annually, is highly dependent on healthy beaches, coral reefs, and coastal ecosystems. Rising sea levels and ecosystem degradation could reduce this revenue.

5. Economic Impact of Species Extinctions

- **Keystone Species Loss**: The extinction of keystone species—those that play a critical role in maintaining ecosystem stability—can lead to cascading effects throughout ecosystems, further degrading ecosystem services. For example, the extinction of pollinators or apex predators can result in the collapse of entire ecosystems.

  - **Economic Impact**: The extinction of economically valuable species (e.g., fisheries, pollinators, medicinal plants) will directly affect industries such as agriculture, fisheries, and pharmaceuticals, resulting in billions of dollars in lost revenue.

- **Reduced Genetic Diversity**: Biodiversity provides genetic diversity, which is essential for agricultural resilience, breeding programs, and the development of new crops that can withstand climate change. The loss of biodiversity will reduce the genetic pool available for crop development, increasing the vulnerability of global food systems to pests, diseases, and changing climate conditions.

6. Increased Vulnerability to Natural Disasters

- **Loss of Natural Buffers**: Ecosystems like forests, wetlands, and coral reefs act as natural buffers against extreme weather events such as hurricanes, floods, and landslides. As these ecosystems degrade, communities become more vulnerable to natural disasters, increasing the economic costs of recovery and rebuilding.
  - **Economic Impact**: The loss of natural disaster buffers could result in billions of dollars in additional damage annually, particularly in coastal and forested regions that rely on ecosystems for protection.

7. Impact on Indigenous and Local Communities

- **Loss of Livelihoods**: Many indigenous and local communities depend on biodiversity and ecosystems for their livelihoods, through activities like fishing, hunting, gathering, and small-scale agriculture. The degradation of these ecosystems will lead to economic losses for these communities, exacerbating poverty and inequality.

- **Cultural and Spiritual Loss**: For many communities, biodiversity and ecosystems hold cultural, spiritual, and traditional significance. The loss of these natural systems can result in the loss of cultural identity and traditional knowledge, which has an intangible economic and social cost.

8. Adaptation Costs

- **Restoration and Conservation Efforts**: As ecosystems degrade, governments and businesses will need to invest more in conservation, restoration, and adaptation measures to preserve biodiversity and maintain ecosystem services. These efforts, while necessary, will come with significant costs.
    - **Economic Impact**: Global efforts to restore ecosystems and protect biodiversity could require hundreds of billions of dollars in investment over the coming decades, diverting resources from other areas of the economy.
- **Sustainable Resource Management**: Transitioning to more sustainable practices in agriculture, forestry, and fisheries will require upfront investment in technology, education, and infrastructure. While these practices can help mitigate biodiversity loss, the economic transition may come with short-term disruptions and costs.

Summary

The loss of biodiversity and ecosystem services will have profound economic consequences across various sectors, including agriculture, fisheries, forestry, tourism, and healthcare. Ecosystems provide essential services that support food production, regulate water supplies, protect against natural disasters, and help mitigate climate change. As biodiversity declines and ecosystems degrade, the costs of replacing or losing these services will rise, putting additional strain on global economies and reducing resilience to future climate impacts.

Migration and displacement

Migration and displacement due to climate change represent significant socioeconomic and humanitarian challenges with substantial economic costs. As rising temperatures, extreme weather events, and environmental degradation force people to leave their homes, the movement of populations will disrupt labor markets, strain resources, and create tensions in host regions. Below is an analysis of the economic and social impacts of climate-induced migration and displacement.

1. Causes of Climate-Induced Migration

- **Rising Sea Levels**: Coastal areas and low-lying islands are particularly vulnerable to sea-level rise. Populations living in areas like Bangladesh, the Maldives, and coastal U.S. cities will be forced to relocate as their homes become uninhabitable due to flooding and erosion.
- **Extreme Weather Events**: Hurricanes, floods, wildfires, and droughts are becoming more frequent and severe due to climate change, leading to both short-term displacements and long-term migrations. For example, hurricanes in the Caribbean and wildfires in California have displaced thousands of people in recent years.
- **Desertification and Drought**: In regions like Sub-Saharan Africa, the Middle East, and South Asia, increasing temperatures and prolonged droughts are making agricultural livelihoods unsustainable, leading to migration from rural areas to urban centers or across borders.

- **Resource Scarcity**: Water shortages, declining agricultural productivity, and competition over dwindling natural resources can lead to social and political tensions, forcing people to migrate in search of better opportunities and living conditions.

2. Scale of the Problem

- The **World Bank** estimates that by 2050, climate change could displace up to **216 million people** across six regions: Sub-Saharan Africa, South Asia, East Asia and the Pacific, Latin America, North Africa, and Eastern Europe and Central Asia.
- These migrations are typically internal, with people moving from rural areas to cities, but there are also significant cross-border movements. For instance, migration flows from Central America to the U.S. are increasingly driven by climate-related factors like drought and hurricanes.
- In small island developing states (SIDS), entire populations may need to be relocated as sea levels rise, creating "climate refugees."

3. Economic Costs of Migration and Displacement

- **Impact on Host Regions**:
    - **Strain on Public Services**: In regions receiving large numbers of migrants, especially urban areas, there will be increased demand for housing, healthcare, education, and other public services. Local governments will need to invest more in infrastructure to accommodate the growing population, leading to higher public spending.

  - **Unemployment and Social Tensions**: Migrants often compete for jobs with local populations, which can lead to higher unemployment rates and wage suppression, especially in low-skilled sectors. This can also exacerbate tensions between migrants and local communities, leading to social unrest and instability.
  - **Housing Shortages**: Rapid population growth in urban centers due to migration can lead to overcrowded cities, housing shortages, and the expansion of informal settlements. In many cases, slum areas lack adequate sanitation, healthcare, and access to clean water, increasing the vulnerability of migrant populations to disease and poverty.
  - **Increase in Poverty**: Many climate migrants come from rural, agricultural backgrounds and may lack the skills needed to integrate into urban economies. This often results in higher levels of poverty and economic exclusion among migrant communities.
- **Impact on Sending Regions**:
  - **Loss of Labor Force**: In regions that experience large outflows of migrants, particularly rural areas, the departure of the working-age population can lead to labor shortages, reduced agricultural production, and economic decline. This can further exacerbate poverty and food insecurity in these regions.
  - **Erosion of Local Economies**: Climate-induced migration can disrupt local economies, as people are forced to abandon their homes, farms, and businesses. This economic dislocation reduces productivity and

increases the dependency on aid, which creates a vicious cycle of poverty and underdevelopment.

4. Social and Humanitarian Impacts

- **Human Rights Challenges**: Climate-induced migrants often face legal and social challenges in their host regions, particularly because international law does not currently recognize "climate refugees." This leaves them without formal protection under existing refugee frameworks, making it harder to access legal rights, work permits, or social services.
- **Health and Well-being**: Displaced populations are more vulnerable to health problems due to poor living conditions in temporary shelters or informal settlements. These conditions can lead to the spread of communicable diseases, malnutrition, and mental health issues like trauma and stress from displacement.
- **Education Disruptions**: Children in displaced families often face interruptions in their education, which can have long-term consequences on human capital development and economic productivity in the future.

5. Regional Variations

- **Sub-Saharan Africa**: This region is one of the most vulnerable to climate-induced migration due to its high dependence on rain-fed agriculture and frequent droughts. By 2050, an estimated **85 million people** could be displaced within the region, with migration flows moving from rural areas toward cities like Lagos, Nairobi, and Kinshasa.
- **South Asia**: Rising sea levels and increasing temperatures will make parts of South Asia uninhabitable, particularly in Bangladesh, where more than **13 million people** are at risk of

displacement. India will also face significant internal migration as droughts and heatwaves make farming in regions like the Ganges Basin more difficult.

- **Pacific Islands**: Small island nations like Tuvalu, Kiribati, and the Maldives are particularly at risk of total displacement due to rising sea levels. Entire populations may need to relocate to other countries, such as New Zealand or Australia, which will involve complex international negotiations and legal frameworks for resettlement.

6. Impact on Global Economies

- **Pressure on International Aid and Humanitarian Systems**: The growing number of climate refugees will place increasing pressure on international aid organizations and humanitarian systems. Countries and organizations will need to provide more funding for disaster relief, temporary shelters, and infrastructure rebuilding in both source and host regions.
    - **Example**: In 2020, the **UNHCR** (United Nations High Commissioner for Refugees) reported that nearly **30 million people** were displaced by natural disasters alone, requiring significant international aid to provide shelter and services.
- **Trade and Economic Stability**: Migration driven by climate change can also disrupt trade, especially in regions that rely on agriculture or fisheries. For example, as smallholder farmers abandon their land, food production decreases, leading to higher food prices and inflation, which can destabilize economies, especially in low-income countries.
- **Impact on Labor Markets**: While migration can provide an economic boost by adding to the labor force in receiving regions, it can also strain local labor markets, especially in

developing countries with limited job opportunities. In some cases, migrant laborers can help drive economic growth in sectors like construction, agriculture, and services, but this is highly dependent on policies and infrastructure in place to integrate migrants.

7. Political and Security Implications

- **Conflict over Resources**: In many cases, climate-induced migration exacerbates tensions over scarce resources like water, land, and food. As populations move into new areas, competition for these resources can lead to conflict between migrants and local communities.
    - **Example**: In the Sahel region of Africa, desertification and drought have contributed to violent conflicts between farmers and herders over access to water and grazing land. This has forced many people to migrate, further destabilizing the region.
- **Political Instability**: Large-scale migration can fuel political instability, particularly in countries where governments are already weak or fragile. The movement of displaced populations across borders can lead to tensions between countries, especially if migration is seen as a threat to national security or economic stability.
- **Rise of Populism and Xenophobia**: In many countries, the arrival of climate migrants can contribute to the rise of populist and xenophobic political movements. These movements often exploit fears about competition for jobs, housing, and social services to stoke anti-immigrant sentiment, which can undermine social cohesion and political stability.

8. Adaptation and Mitigation Measures

- **Investment in Resilient Infrastructure**: To reduce the economic and social costs of displacement, governments will need to invest in climate-resilient infrastructure, particularly in vulnerable coastal and agricultural regions. This includes building sea walls, improving water management systems, and developing drought-resistant crops to reduce the need for migration.
- **Legal and Policy Frameworks**: There is a growing need for international legal frameworks that recognize and protect climate refugees. These frameworks should ensure that displaced populations have access to legal rights, social services, and safe resettlement options.
- **Planned Relocation Programs**: Some countries are beginning to implement planned relocation programs for populations in high-risk areas. These programs aim to move communities in a controlled and sustainable manner before climate impacts force sudden and chaotic migrations.

Summary

Climate change-induced migration and displacement will have far-reaching economic, social, and political impacts. As millions of people are forced to relocate due to rising sea levels, extreme weather, and resource scarcity, the strain on host regions, the loss of labor in source regions, and the costs of humanitarian assistance will increase. To address these challenges, governments, international organizations, and the private sector must work together to develop policies that protect vulnerable populations, promote sustainable development, and ensure that migration is managed in an equitable and orderly way.

Energy Transition and Decarbonization

Energy transition and decarbonization are key components of the global response to climate change, but they come with significant economic costs and challenges. Shifting from fossil fuels to cleaner energy sources is essential to limit global warming to below 2°C, as agreed in the Paris Agreement. The transition requires investments in renewable energy, electrification, energy efficiency, and new technologies, but it also involves economic disruptions in industries reliant on fossil fuels.

Here's a breakdown of the key components and costs associated with the energy transition and decarbonization:

1. Investment in Renewable Energy

- **Renewable Energy Infrastructure**: To replace fossil fuels, massive investments are needed in renewable energy infrastructure such as solar, wind, hydro, and geothermal power plants. This includes the cost of building power plants, upgrading transmission grids, and developing energy storage solutions.
    - **Cost Estimates**: The International Renewable Energy Agency (IRENA) estimates that global investments in renewable energy need to reach **$110 trillion** by 2050 to meet climate goals. These investments include the expansion of solar and wind farms, as well as storage technologies to address the intermittency of renewables.
- **Energy Storage and Grid Modernization**: Since renewable energy sources like wind and solar are intermittent, significant investments in energy storage (e.g., batteries, pumped hydro storage) are required to ensure a stable power supply.

Upgrading power grids to handle decentralized and fluctuating power generation is also crucial.

  - **Cost Impact**: The **International Energy Agency (IEA)** estimates that around **$6 trillion** in investments will be needed by 2050 to modernize the grid and develop energy storage capacity. This will include everything from smart grids to demand-response technologies.

- **Decentralized Energy Systems**: In developing countries and remote areas, the energy transition will involve the deployment of decentralized, off-grid renewable energy systems. These systems can provide electricity to communities that are not connected to the national grid.

  - **Impact**: Decentralized systems are crucial for reducing energy poverty and can provide a more sustainable and resilient energy supply in rural and remote regions. However, the initial costs of deploying these systems are high.

2. Decarbonizing Industry and Transportation

- **Electrification of Transportation**: One of the major components of decarbonization is the shift to electric vehicles (EVs) and public transport systems powered by clean energy. This involves building new EV charging infrastructure, producing batteries, and transitioning from internal combustion engine (ICE) vehicles to electric.

  - **Cost Estimates**: The IEA estimates that achieving net-zero emissions in the transportation sector by 2050 will require an investment of **$3.5 trillion** globally, which includes the electrification of vehicles and infrastructure upgrades.

- **Decarbonizing Heavy Industry**: Sectors like steel, cement, and chemicals are among the most challenging to decarbonize due to their high reliance on fossil fuels and energy-intensive processes. To reduce emissions, these industries need to adopt new technologies such as hydrogen-based processes, carbon capture and storage (CCS), and electrification.
    - **Cost Estimates**: Decarbonizing the global industrial sector could require up to **$20 trillion** in investment by 2050. This includes retrofitting existing facilities with CCS technologies, switching to low-carbon materials, and adopting new production processes.
- **Hydrogen Economy**: Hydrogen is emerging as a key fuel for decarbonizing industries that are difficult to electrify, such as aviation, shipping, and heavy manufacturing. Developing a hydrogen economy will require investments in hydrogen production, storage, and distribution infrastructure.
    - **Cost of Hydrogen Transition**: The IEA estimates that achieving widespread adoption of hydrogen technologies could require between **$1-2 trillion** in global investment by 2050.

3. Energy Efficiency

- **Building Retrofitting**: Retrofitting existing buildings to improve energy efficiency is a critical part of reducing emissions. This involves upgrading insulation, installing energy-efficient windows and appliances, and adopting smart energy management systems.
    - **Cost of Energy Efficiency Measures**: According to the Global Alliance for Buildings and Construction, improving energy efficiency in the building sector could require investments of **$5 trillion** by 2050.

These measures are essential for reducing the energy consumption of homes, offices, and factories.

- **Energy-Efficient Manufacturing**: Industries will need to adopt energy-efficient technologies and practices, such as optimizing production processes, using energy-efficient equipment, and minimizing waste.
    - **Cost Impact**: Improving energy efficiency in industrial processes could result in **$2-4 trillion** in investments by 2050, depending on the sector and region.

4. Carbon Capture, Utilization, and Storage (CCUS)

- **Carbon Capture Technologies**: CCUS is considered essential for achieving net-zero emissions, particularly for sectors like cement and steel, which are difficult to decarbonize through electrification alone. Carbon capture technologies involve capturing CO2 emissions from power plants and industrial facilities and either storing it underground or using it in other processes.
    - **Cost of CCUS**: The IEA estimates that CCUS deployment will require **$1.6 trillion** in investment by 2050 to capture and store over 7 gigatons of CO2 annually.
- **Utilization of Captured Carbon**: Captured CO2 can be used in various industries, such as producing synthetic fuels, chemicals, or materials like concrete. However, the market for these products is still in its early stages, and scaling up utilization technologies will require significant investment.
    - **Potential Market**: The global market for carbon utilization could reach **$1 trillion** by 2050, depending

on the development of new technologies and market demand.

5. Job Creation and Economic Disruption

- **Job Creation in Clean Energy**: The transition to renewable energy and decarbonization is expected to create millions of new jobs in sectors like solar, wind, battery manufacturing, and energy efficiency. According to the IRENA, the renewable energy sector could employ over **42 million people** by 2050, up from around 11 million today.
- **Job Losses in Fossil Fuel Industries**: On the other hand, millions of jobs in coal, oil, and natural gas industries will be lost as these sectors shrink. Managing this transition for workers in fossil fuel-dependent regions will be a significant challenge.
    - **Economic Impact**: The cost of supporting displaced workers, providing retraining programs, and transitioning fossil fuel-dependent communities could be substantial. In the U.S. alone, the cost of transitioning coal workers to new jobs is estimated at **$83 billion** by 2035.
- **Just Transition**: Ensuring a "just transition" for workers and communities affected by the shift away from fossil fuels is crucial for social and political stability. Governments will need to invest in social safety nets, retraining programs, and new economic opportunities to support these regions.

6. Government Policies and Carbon Pricing

- **Subsidies for Clean Energy**: Governments play a critical role in the energy transition by providing subsidies and incentives for renewable energy projects, energy efficiency programs, and research into new technologies. These incentives reduce the upfront costs of clean energy investments and accelerate the transition.

- **Global Subsidy Estimates**: According to the IEA, governments currently provide around **$1 trillion** annually in subsidies for fossil fuels. Redirecting these subsidies toward clean energy could significantly accelerate decarbonization.

- **Carbon Pricing**: Implementing carbon taxes or cap-and-trade systems is an essential policy tool for driving the energy transition. By putting a price on carbon emissions, governments can incentivize companies to reduce their carbon footprint and invest in cleaner technologies.
  - **Cost of Carbon Pricing**: Carbon pricing could generate significant revenue for governments, which can be reinvested in clean energy projects or used to support affected communities. The World Bank estimates that carbon pricing could generate **$4 trillion** annually by 2050.

7. Research, Development, and Innovation

- **Breakthrough Technologies**: Achieving full decarbonization will require the development of new technologies, particularly in areas like energy storage, carbon capture, and hydrogen production. Governments and private companies will need to invest heavily in research and development (R&D) to bring these technologies to market.
  - **Cost of Innovation**: R&D investment in clean energy technologies is expected to exceed **$2 trillion** globally by 2050. This includes the development of next-

generation batteries, advanced nuclear reactors, and sustainable fuels.

8. Global Cooperation and Financial Support

- **Developing Countries**: Many developing countries lack the financial resources and technology to implement the energy transition on their own. Global cooperation and financial support from developed nations will be crucial to help these countries decarbonize while also improving energy access and reducing poverty.
    - **Climate Finance**: The Paris Agreement calls for **$100 billion** per year in climate finance from developed countries to help developing nations mitigate and adapt to climate change. However, actual contributions have fallen short of this target, and much larger sums will be needed in the coming decades.

9. Long-Term Savings and Benefits

- **Avoided Costs from Climate Change**: While the upfront costs of decarbonization are substantial, they are far outweighed by the avoided costs of climate change. By reducing greenhouse gas emissions, the world can avoid trillions of dollars in damages from extreme weather, sea-level rise, and other climate impacts.
    - **Health Benefits**: Decarbonizing energy systems will also lead to significant health benefits by reducing air pollution. This could save millions of lives and reduce healthcare costs related to respiratory diseases, heart conditions, and other pollution-related illnesses.

Losses in tourism and property value due to climate change are significant components of the broader economic impacts of global warming. Rising sea levels, extreme weather events, biodiversity loss, and environmental degradation are already affecting tourist destinations and reducing property values, especially in coastal areas. Below is an analysis of how these factors contribute to the $38 trillion cost of climate change over the next 25 years:

Tourism Losses

Tourism is highly sensitive to environmental conditions, making it particularly vulnerable to climate change. Many of the world's top tourist destinations, such as coastal areas, islands, and natural parks, are at risk from rising temperatures, sea level rise, and other climate impacts. Tourism-dependent economies, especially in developing countries, will suffer from both physical damages and loss of appeal.

a. Sea Level Rise and Coastal Erosion

- **Coastal Destinations at Risk**: Beach resorts, cruise lines, and island destinations are major components of the global tourism industry. Rising sea levels and coastal erosion threaten the very existence of many of these tourist destinations. Popular locations like the Maldives, Seychelles, the Caribbean, and parts of the Mediterranean are seeing beaches shrink, resorts flood, and infrastructure deteriorate.
- **Economic Impact**: The **World Travel & Tourism Council (WTTC)** estimates that climate change could reduce global tourism revenues by **$300 billion annually** by 2050. Coastal tourism, which accounts for nearly 80% of global tourism, is particularly vulnerable. Tourists may choose to avoid regions with damaged beaches or increased risk of hurricanes, further depressing local economies.

b. Damage to Natural Attractions

- **Coral Reefs and Marine Ecosystems**: Coral reefs are among the most valuable natural attractions, supporting tourism, fishing, and coastal protection. However, rising sea temperatures and ocean acidification are causing mass coral bleaching events, which damage these ecosystems. Destinations like Australia's Great Barrier Reef and the Coral Triangle in Southeast Asia are already seeing significant declines in visitors due to coral bleaching.
- **Ecotourism**: Many tourists visit natural parks, glaciers, and wildlife reserves to see biodiversity and unique ecosystems. Climate change, through habitat destruction and species loss, is degrading these attractions. For example, melting glaciers in the Alps and the Himalayas are reducing the appeal of trekking and sightseeing tours, while endangered wildlife, like polar bears and sea turtles, face declining populations.
- **Cost Impact**: The loss of biodiversity and the decline of natural tourist attractions could reduce tourism revenues by **$100 billion annually** by 2050, affecting countries that rely on ecotourism, such as Costa Rica, Kenya, and Madagascar.

c. Extreme Weather Events

- **Hurricanes, Floods, and Wildfires**: Destinations prone to extreme weather events are seeing increased risks, making them less attractive to tourists. Hurricanes in the Caribbean, wildfires in California and Australia, and floods in Southeast Asia disrupt travel plans, damage infrastructure, and deter future visitors. Resorts and hotels in hurricane-prone areas face higher insurance premiums and rebuilding costs, further straining local tourism industries.

- **Heatwaves**: Rising temperatures are making certain destinations less comfortable for travelers. Mediterranean countries like Spain, Italy, and Greece are experiencing more frequent heatwaves during the peak summer season, causing tourists to avoid these areas and choose cooler destinations instead.

- **Cost to Local Economies**: Extreme weather-related damages to tourism infrastructure, along with reduced visitor numbers, could cause losses of up to **$50 billion annually** by 2050, particularly affecting coastal and island nations.

2. Loss of Property Value

Property markets, especially in coastal and vulnerable regions, are heavily impacted by climate change. Rising sea levels, increased flooding, and extreme weather events can lead to significant declines in property values, insurance premiums, and overall economic stability in affected areas.

a. Coastal Property and Sea Level Rise

- **Flood Risk**: Sea level rise is perhaps the most direct threat to property values in coastal regions. As water encroaches on land, properties in areas like Florida, Louisiana, the Netherlands, and Southeast Asia are at greater risk of flooding. Regular flooding and the inability to secure insurance make these properties less desirable, leading to a decrease in market value.

- **Example**: A study by the **Union of Concerned Scientists** estimated that over **$1 trillion** in U.S. coastal property could be at risk by 2100 due to sea level rise, particularly in states like Florida, where real estate markets are highly dependent on waterfront properties. Globally, this number is even higher, as countries like Bangladesh, Vietnam, and Indonesia face severe inundation risks.

- **Insurance Implications**: As climate risks increase, insurance companies are raising premiums or pulling coverage from high-risk areas altogether. This further devalues properties, as buyers are unwilling to invest in assets that they cannot insure against climate impacts.
- **Economic Loss**: Property devaluation and loss of insurability in high-risk coastal areas could result in global losses exceeding **$5 trillion** by 2050, as more properties are classified as uninhabitable or abandoned due to climate-related risks.

b. Wildfires and Extreme Weather

- **Fire-Prone Regions**: Regions prone to wildfires, like California, Australia, and the Mediterranean, are seeing reduced property values as fire risk grows. Entire communities can be wiped out by wildfires, as seen in California's Camp Fire and Australia's 2020 wildfires. In these regions, properties face skyrocketing insurance premiums, reduced buyer interest, and large-scale property abandonment.
- **Storm-Prone Areas**: Hurricanes, typhoons, and severe storms can destroy homes and infrastructure, leading to costly rebuilds. Areas like the Gulf Coast in the U.S., the Caribbean, and parts of Southeast Asia are particularly vulnerable. The increased frequency and severity of these storms are causing investors to shy away from developing in these areas, depressing property values.

- **Cost Impact**: The total property losses from extreme weather events (wildfires, hurricanes, storms) could exceed **$1 trillion** globally by 2050, with significant regional impacts in high-risk areas.

c. Heatwaves and Agricultural Decline

- **Urban Areas**: Rising temperatures are making certain cities less livable, reducing property values in urban areas that face extreme heat. Heatwaves can damage infrastructure, reduce energy efficiency, and increase the cost of living. Cities in Southern Europe, the Middle East, and South Asia are seeing declining interest in real estate as summer temperatures soar to unbearable levels.
- **Agricultural Land**: Climate change is also devaluing agricultural land, particularly in regions experiencing droughts and desertification. Farmers in regions like California's Central Valley, the Sahel, and Southern Europe are seeing their land lose value as water scarcity and soil degradation make farming less viable.
- **Cost Impact**: The loss of agricultural land value could amount to **$200 billion** globally by 2050, particularly affecting regions that depend on farming as a key economic driver.

3. Adaptation Costs for Tourism and Property Markets

- **Protective Measures**: In response to rising risks, some regions are investing heavily in adaptation measures like seawalls, flood barriers, and climate-resilient infrastructure. For example, cities like Miami and New York are spending billions to protect against sea level rise and storm surges, while ski resorts are investing in snow-making technologies to cope with declining snowfall. However, these adaptation measures are expensive and do not guarantee long-term protection.

- **Cost of Adaptation**: The **World Bank** estimates that climate adaptation in cities could cost up to **$80-100 billion** annually by 2030, including measures to protect tourism infrastructure and property in high-risk areas.

- **Rebuilding Costs**: After extreme weather events, the cost of rebuilding hotels, resorts, and homes can be substantial. Governments, insurers, and property owners are bearing increasingly higher costs for reconstruction. For example, in the aftermath of Hurricane Maria, Puerto Rico faced over **$90 billion** in damages, much of it related to destroyed homes and tourist infrastructure.

4. Long-Term Economic Implications

- **Reduced Investment**: As climate risks increase, investors are becoming more cautious about putting money into vulnerable regions, particularly in tourism and real estate markets. Coastal areas, once considered prime real estate, are becoming high-risk investments, leading to a withdrawal of capital from these markets.

- **Tourism Dependency**: Countries that rely heavily on tourism for economic growth, such as small island nations and coastal regions, face significant long-term economic decline. The loss of tourism revenue could lead to a reduction in GDP, increased unemployment, and higher levels of poverty.

- **Global Economic Impact**: Combined, the losses in tourism and property value could reduce global economic output by over **$3 trillion** by 2050. These losses will be concentrated in regions with high climate vulnerability, exacerbating inequality between rich and poor countries.

Summary

The losses in tourism and property value are major components of the projected cost of climate change over the next 25 years. Rising sea levels, extreme weather events, and environmental degradation will significantly impact coastal and nature-based tourism, while property values in high-risk areas will plummet due to increased flooding, wildfires, and heatwaves. Adaptation efforts can mitigate some of these impacts, but the long-term economic consequences are substantial and will disproportionately affect regions highly dependent on tourism and real estate.

Chapter Five
Fossil Fuel Industry's Strategies to Offset Revenue Losses Due to Global Warming

Introduction

The global fossil fuel industry, a key driver of the world's energy supply, is facing significant challenges due to global warming, shifting public perceptions, stricter environmental regulations, and the rise of renewable energy alternatives. As governments and businesses pivot toward carbon neutrality to mitigate climate change, demand for fossil fuels—especially coal and oil—is expected to decline over the coming decades. In response, the fossil fuel industry is exploring a variety of strategies to offset potential revenue losses. These strategies include diversifying into renewable energy, investing in carbon capture and storage (CCS) technologies, and leveraging new markets such as hydrogen and biofuels. This report provides an

1. Diversification into Renewable Energy

As global pressure mounts to transition to cleaner energy sources, many fossil fuel companies have begun diversifying into renewable energy. This strategic shift allows them to hedge against declining demand for fossil fuels and capitalize on the growing demand for sustainable energy solutions. Companies that traditionally relied on oil, gas, and coal are now exploring various renewable energy sources, particularly solar and wind power.

Solar and Wind Power Investments

- **Shell**: Shell has committed to becoming a net-zero emissions energy company by 2050. A key part of this plan involves expanding its renewable energy portfolio. Shell has invested in large solar power projects, including its acquisition of solar energy companies such as Silicon Ranch in the U.S. Additionally, Shell is involved in offshore and onshore wind power development. Its acquisition of EOLFI, a French wind energy firm, showcases its dedication to tapping into the offshore wind market.

- **BP**: British Petroleum (BP) has set a goal to reduce its oil and gas output by 40% by 2030 and increase its low-carbon investments tenfold. BP is pursuing large-scale renewable energy projects, including offshore wind farms in the U.K. and the U.S. The company is also heavily invested in solar power through its subsidiary, Lightsource BP, one of the world's leading solar developers.

- **TotalEnergies**: TotalEnergies (formerly Total) has rebranded itself to reflect its commitment to becoming a broader energy company, not just an oil producer. The company is heavily invested in renewable energy sources such as solar, wind, and batteries. By 2030, TotalEnergies aims to generate 100 gigawatts (GW) of renewable energy capacity, with a focus on both solar and offshore wind projects globally.

Acquisition of Renewable Energy Startups

One of the key methods these companies are using to expand into the renewable energy sector is acquiring startups and companies already established in the renewable space. This approach allows them to quickly scale their renewable energy capabilities without needing to build expertise from scratch.

- **Chevron**: Chevron has been expanding its renewable energy portfolio by investing in startups that specialize in next-generation biofuels and carbon capture technologies. Chevron's partnership with Brightmark, a waste-to-energy company, demonstrates its commitment to renewable fuels made from waste plastics and organic materials.
- **ExxonMobil**: ExxonMobil, traditionally slow to move into renewables compared to its competitors, has started investing in clean energy technology through its Low Carbon Solutions business unit. While ExxonMobil's investments are still heavily focused on carbon capture and hydrogen, the company has also shown interest in renewable energy technologies like wind and solar.

Long-Term Energy Transition Goals

The diversification efforts of the fossil fuel industry are closely tied to their long-term energy transition goals. Many companies have announced ambitious plans to achieve net-zero emissions by 2050 or sooner, aligning with the Paris Agreement's climate targets. These commitments require a dramatic shift in their energy portfolios away from fossil fuels and towards renewables, energy efficiency, and cleaner technologies.

In conclusion, the diversification into renewable energy is a crucial pillar of the fossil fuel industry's strategy to offset revenue loss and remain competitive in the evolving energy landscape. By investing in solar and wind power, acquiring renewable startups, and committing to long-term sustainability goals, fossil fuel companies are beginning to reposition themselves as energy companies focused on a low-carbon future. However, the scale and speed of these transitions will determine their ability to succeed in a world increasingly moving away from fossil fuels.

2. Investing in Carbon Capture and Storage (CCS)

Carbon capture and storage (CCS) has emerged as a critical technology for the fossil fuel industry to address the growing demand for reducing carbon emissions while continuing fossil fuel operations. By capturing carbon dioxide (CO_2) emissions from industrial sources and storing them underground or utilizing them in other processes, CCS can significantly reduce the environmental impact of fossil fuel-based energy. Many fossil fuel companies are investing in CCS technologies as part of their strategy to offset potential revenue losses from the transition to a low-carbon economy.

Overview of Carbon Capture and Storage (CCS)

CCS involves three main steps:

1. **Capturing** CO_2 from large point sources, such as power plants or industrial facilities.
2. **Transporting** the captured CO_2 to a storage site, typically through pipelines.
3. **Storing** the CO_2 underground in geological formations such as depleted oil and gas fields or deep saline aquifers, where it can be permanently isolated from the atmosphere.

Alternatively, captured carbon can be used in various industrial processes, including enhanced oil recovery (EOR), which involves injecting CO_2 into oil fields to extract additional oil. This use of captured CO_2 offers a financial incentive for oil companies while contributing to emissions reduction.

Key Investments in CCS by Fossil Fuel Companies

Several fossil fuel companies are leading efforts to develop and deploy large-scale CCS projects. These companies see CCS as an essential tool to allow continued fossil fuel production while meeting global climate goals.

- **ExxonMobil**: ExxonMobil is one of the largest investors in CCS technology. The company has made significant investments in CCS research and development, with plans to capture over 100 million metric tons of CO_2 annually by 2040. In 2021, ExxonMobil proposed a large-scale CCS hub in Houston, Texas, aiming to store CO_2 emissions from industrial facilities along the Gulf Coast. The company envisions this project as a key contributor to reducing industrial emissions in one of the most carbon-intensive regions in the U.S.

- **Chevron**: Chevron has been actively pursuing CCS initiatives, particularly through its Gorgon Project in Australia. The Gorgon CCS project, one of the world's largest, captures CO_2 from natural gas processing operations and stores it in a deep underground reservoir. Since its start in 2019, Chevron has captured and stored millions of tons of CO_2, contributing to Australia's climate targets.

- **Shell**: Shell is also a significant player in the CCS space. The company operates the Quest CCS project in Alberta, Canada, which captures CO_2 from its oil sands operations and stores it underground. Quest has successfully stored over 6 million tons of CO_2 since its launch in 2015. Additionally, Shell is involved in various CCS research collaborations and has committed to expanding its CCS projects globally, including a partnership with Norway's Northern Lights CCS project.

- **BP**: BP is investing in CCS technologies as part of its broader strategy to reduce carbon emissions. The company has partnered with Equinor and National Grid to develop the Net Zero Teesside project in the U.K., which aims to capture and store CO_2 emissions from local industrial facilities. BP views

CCS as critical to decarbonizing heavy industries, such as steel and cement, where emissions are harder to eliminate through electrification alone.

Partnerships and Collaboration with Governments

In addition to internal investments, fossil fuel companies are partnering with governments and international organizations to scale CCS deployment. Many governments are providing financial incentives and regulatory support for CCS projects to meet national and global climate targets.

- **Public-Private Partnerships**: For example, the U.S. government has committed funding to support CCS projects, with legislation like the 45Q tax credit, which provides financial incentives for capturing and storing CO_2. ExxonMobil, Chevron, and other major fossil fuel companies have actively lobbied for the expansion of such incentives to make CCS more economically viable.
- **International Collaboration**: In Europe, fossil fuel companies are collaborating with governments to develop CCS infrastructure, such as the Northern Lights project in Norway, which is supported by Equinor, Shell, and TotalEnergies. The project aims to create a large-scale CCS network across Europe, with the potential to store CO_2 from various industries in countries that lack suitable geological storage sites.

Challenges Facing CCS Deployment

While CCS holds promise, several challenges could hinder its large-scale adoption:

- **High Costs**: CCS is still relatively expensive compared to other emissions reduction technologies, such as renewable energy. The costs of capturing, transporting, and storing CO_2 need to decrease significantly for CCS to become widely adopted.

- **Limited Infrastructure**: Developing the infrastructure necessary to transport and store CO_2 on a large scale presents logistical and financial challenges. For CCS to scale globally, countries will need to invest heavily in pipelines and storage facilities, often with government support.
- **Public Perception**: There is skepticism from environmental groups and the public regarding CCS. Critics argue that CCS may perpetuate the use of fossil fuels by offering a technological fix rather than encouraging a full transition to renewable energy.

The Role of CCS in the Energy Transition

Despite these challenges, CCS is seen by many experts as an essential tool for reducing emissions from industries that are difficult to decarbonize, such as steel, cement, and petrochemicals. For the fossil fuel industry, CCS offers a way to continue using fossil fuels while aligning with international climate commitments. By investing in CCS, fossil fuel companies can reduce their carbon footprint and potentially generate new revenue streams by selling captured CO_2 for industrial uses, such as EOR or carbonated products.

Conclusion

Investing in carbon capture and storage (CCS) is a central strategy for fossil fuel companies seeking to offset revenue losses due to the global energy transition. By capturing and storing CO_2 emissions from industrial processes and energy production, companies like ExxonMobil, Shell, BP, and Chevron are positioning themselves as leaders in emissions reduction technologies. However, the success of CCS on a global scale will depend on overcoming challenges related to cost, infrastructure, and public perception, as well as continued collaboration between the private sector and governments to create the necessary regulatory frameworks and financial incentives.

New Markets: Hydrogen and Biofuels

In response to global decarbonization efforts and the declining long-term demand for traditional fossil fuels, companies in the fossil fuel industry are increasingly exploring new markets to diversify their revenue streams. Two of the most promising areas are **hydrogen energy** and **biofuels**, both of which are considered key components of a sustainable, low-carbon future. These markets offer fossil fuel companies opportunities to leverage existing infrastructure and expertise while aligning with global climate goals.

Hydrogen Energy

Hydrogen is emerging as a critical energy source in the transition to a low-carbon economy, with potential applications in sectors where direct electrification is challenging, such as heavy industry, transportation, and heating. Fossil fuel companies are investing in both **blue hydrogen** (produced from natural gas with carbon capture and storage) and **green hydrogen** (produced using renewable electricity to split water into hydrogen and oxygen).

Types of Hydrogen

- **Blue Hydrogen**: Produced from natural gas, blue hydrogen involves capturing the carbon emissions produced during the process and storing them through carbon capture and storage (CCS). This allows fossil fuel companies to utilize their existing natural gas assets while reducing carbon emissions.
- **Green Hydrogen**: Produced using electrolysis powered by renewable energy (such as wind or solar), green hydrogen is considered the cleanest form of hydrogen. Though more

expensive to produce, it is seen as the ultimate goal in the hydrogen economy.

Key Investments in Hydrogen by Fossil Fuel Companies

- **Shell**: Shell has invested heavily in hydrogen projects worldwide, viewing hydrogen as an important part of its clean energy strategy. In 2021, Shell joined a consortium to develop a major green hydrogen project in the Netherlands, using offshore wind to power the electrolysis process. Additionally, Shell is investing in hydrogen refueling infrastructure for vehicles, positioning itself as a leader in the hydrogen fuel cell market for transportation.

- **BP**: BP is exploring both blue and green hydrogen opportunities as part of its commitment to reduce emissions. The company has partnered with industrial players in the U.K. to develop the Teesside hydrogen project, which aims to produce up to 1 gigawatt (GW) of blue hydrogen by 2030. BP is also exploring green hydrogen production at its refineries in Europe, where it can integrate renewable electricity into its hydrogen production processes.

- **Chevron**: Chevron is positioning itself as a key player in the hydrogen market by investing in both production and distribution infrastructure. The company has partnered with Toyota to explore hydrogen fueling stations and has invested in several hydrogen production facilities globally, focusing on blue hydrogen with CCS.

Hydrogen's Role in the Energy Transition

Hydrogen is particularly attractive for its versatility, as it can be used in several applications:

- **Transportation**: Hydrogen fuel cells are seen as an alternative to batteries for heavy-duty vehicles like trucks, buses, and ships.
- **Industry**: Hydrogen is a potential solution for decarbonizing industrial sectors such as steel and cement, where direct electrification is more difficult.
- **Power Generation**: Hydrogen can be used in power plants as a fuel to generate electricity, either on its own or blended with natural gas, with the added advantage of producing zero carbon emissions when used as fuel.

Biofuels

Biofuels represent another promising market for fossil fuel companies, particularly for industries where alternative energy sources, such as electric batteries, are less feasible. Biofuels are derived from organic materials, such as plant biomass, animal waste, and used cooking oil, and can be used to replace conventional fossil fuels in transportation, aviation, and shipping.

Types of Biofuels

- **First-Generation Biofuels**: Derived from food crops such as corn (ethanol) and vegetable oils (biodiesel), these biofuels are widely used but have faced criticism due to competition with food production and potential negative environmental impacts.

- **Second-Generation Biofuels**: Produced from non-food biomass, such as agricultural residues, forestry waste, and dedicated energy crops, second-generation biofuels are seen as more sustainable than their first-generation counterparts.
- **Third-Generation Biofuels**: These biofuels are derived from algae and other microorganisms, which can grow quickly and produce high yields of bio-oil, making them a promising future alternative.

Key Investments in Biofuels by Fossil Fuel Companies

- **Chevron**: Chevron has been expanding its biofuel production capabilities as part of its broader strategy to provide cleaner fuels for the transportation sector. In partnership with agribusiness giant Bunge, Chevron is producing renewable diesel from soybeans and other plant-based feedstocks. Chevron is also exploring advanced biofuels made from algae, which could provide a long-term, scalable alternative to traditional biodiesel.
- **ExxonMobil**: ExxonMobil has been a major proponent of algae-based biofuels, investing hundreds of millions of dollars in research and development. The company has partnered with biotech firms to explore the commercial viability of algae biofuels, which have the potential to produce large volumes of energy-dense fuel without competing with food crops.
- **Shell**: Shell has invested in various biofuel projects, including advanced biofuels made from waste materials. In Brazil, Shell operates one of the largest ethanol production plants in partnership with local sugarcane growers. Ethanol produced from sugarcane is a key biofuel for transportation in the country, and Shell sees biofuels as a major growth area in global markets where electrification is not viable.

- **TotalEnergies**: TotalEnergies has made significant investments in biofuels, particularly for the aviation sector. The company recently converted a refinery in France to produce renewable diesel and aviation biofuels from waste and biomass, positioning itself as a leader in sustainable fuel solutions for the airline industry.

Biofuels' Role in the Energy Transition

Biofuels are critical for decarbonizing sectors that cannot be easily electrified:

- **Aviation**: Sustainable aviation fuels (SAFs), which are biofuels made from waste materials, are seen as one of the few viable options for reducing emissions from air travel in the near term.
- **Shipping**: Biofuels can be used to power ships, helping reduce the carbon footprint of the shipping industry, which currently relies heavily on fossil fuels.
- **Heavy-Duty Transportation**: Renewable diesel and biodiesel offer immediate alternatives to conventional diesel in trucks and buses, providing a near-term solution for reducing emissions in the transport sector.

Challenges and Opportunities

While hydrogen and biofuels present significant opportunities for fossil fuel companies, there are challenges to their large-scale adoption:

- **Cost Competitiveness**: The cost of producing green hydrogen and advanced biofuels remains high compared to fossil fuels. For hydrogen, lowering the cost of electrolysis and increasing the availability of renewable energy will be critical to scaling production. Similarly, biofuels need to become more cost-competitive with conventional fuels, especially as demand for sustainable aviation and shipping fuels increases.

- **Infrastructure**: Scaling hydrogen production and distribution requires significant investment in new infrastructure, such as pipelines and refueling stations. For biofuels, existing infrastructure can be repurposed to some extent, but further development is necessary to meet growing demand.
- **Policy and Regulation**: Government incentives, such as carbon pricing, tax credits, and mandates for renewable fuels, are crucial for supporting hydrogen and biofuel markets. Policies that promote the adoption of these technologies, such as the U.S. Renewable Fuel Standard and the European Union's Renewable Energy Directive, will drive investment and demand.

Conclusion

Entering new markets like hydrogen and biofuels allows fossil fuel companies to diversify their portfolios and capture new revenue streams as the world moves toward decarbonization. Hydrogen, with its versatility and potential to decarbonize heavy industry, transportation, and power generation, is emerging as a major area of growth for companies like Shell, BP, and Chevron. Biofuels, particularly in the aviation and shipping sectors, offer an immediate alternative to fossil fuels and provide a sustainable solution for reducing emissions in sectors that are difficult to electrify. However, the industry will need to address challenges related to cost, infrastructure, and policy to realize the full potential of these new energy markets.

4. Digital Transformation and Operational Efficiency

As the fossil fuel industry faces pressure from global decarbonization efforts, rising costs, and increased competition from renewable energy sources, many companies are turning to **digital transformation** to enhance operational efficiency, reduce costs, and maintain profitability. By adopting cutting-edge technologies like artificial intelligence (AI), data analytics, automation, and the Industrial Internet of Things (IIoT), fossil fuel companies are improving asset management, optimizing production, and reducing environmental impacts.

The Role of Digital Transformation

Digital transformation involves integrating digital technologies across operations to improve decision-making, efficiency, and sustainability. For the fossil fuel industry, this transformation allows companies to:

- **Optimize Exploration and Production**: Advanced data analytics and AI enable companies to improve oil and gas exploration, drilling, and production processes. By leveraging real-time data from sensors and satellite imagery, companies can reduce costs and enhance efficiency.
- **Increase Safety and Reduce Environmental Impact**: Automation and IIoT technologies help companies monitor equipment performance, predict maintenance needs, and minimize environmental risks such as oil spills and gas leaks.
- **Lower Operational Costs**: By automating manual processes and streamlining workflows, fossil fuel companies can reduce operating expenses and improve profitability, even as global demand for fossil fuels declines.

Key Digital Technologies Adopted by Fossil Fuel Companies

Artificial Intelligence (AI) and Machine Learning

AI and machine learning are being used to optimize oil and gas operations by processing massive amounts of data and identifying patterns that can enhance production efficiency.

- **Predictive Maintenance**: AI can predict when equipment failures are likely to occur, allowing companies to perform maintenance before breakdowns happen, reducing downtime and repair costs. This is especially critical in offshore oil platforms and refineries, where unscheduled downtime can be extremely costly.
- **Optimizing Drilling and Reservoir Management**: AI helps companies improve the accuracy of reservoir models, optimizing drilling locations and enhancing the recovery of oil and gas from existing fields. AI algorithms analyze geological and seismic data to guide drilling efforts, increasing success rates and reducing costs.
- **ExxonMobil**: ExxonMobil has implemented AI across its upstream operations to optimize reservoir management and boost production efficiency. The company uses machine learning to improve data analysis and decision-making processes, reducing the time and cost associated with exploration.

Industrial Internet of Things (IIoT)

IIoT involves connecting equipment and devices in oil fields, refineries, and pipelines to the internet, allowing companies to collect real-time data, monitor operations remotely, and improve performance.

- **Remote Monitoring and Automation**: IIoT enables real-time monitoring of oil and gas assets, such as wells, pipelines, and refineries, reducing the need for on-site personnel. Automated systems can adjust production levels and optimize energy use based on real-time conditions, helping companies maximize efficiency while minimizing environmental impacts.
- **BP**: BP has integrated IIoT across its global operations to optimize production, monitor equipment health, and enhance safety. Through its "Plant Operations Advisor" system, BP uses data from sensors to monitor equipment in real time and predict maintenance needs.

Big Data and Advanced Analytics

The massive amounts of data generated by the fossil fuel industry, including geological data, production data, and environmental monitoring data, are increasingly being analyzed using advanced analytics to drive better decision-making.

- **Reservoir Management**: Big data analytics are helping companies create more accurate models of underground reservoirs, allowing for more efficient extraction of oil and gas. By integrating data from seismic surveys, production history, and real-time sensors, companies can optimize field development and production strategies.
- **Supply Chain Optimization**: Big data is also improving supply chain management by providing insights into logistics, inventory management, and distribution. Companies can optimize transportation routes, reduce shipping costs, and ensure timely delivery of products to customers.

- **TotalEnergies**: TotalEnergies is using advanced data analytics to improve its operational efficiency and reduce costs. The company's digital initiatives, such as its partnership with Google Cloud to develop AI tools, have helped it optimize exploration and production, enabling more precise decision-making in complex offshore environments.

Cloud Computing and Digital Twins

Cloud computing enables fossil fuel companies to store and process vast amounts of data, making it accessible from anywhere, while **digital twins**—virtual replicas of physical assets—allow for better monitoring and simulation of equipment performance.

- **Digital Twins for Asset Management**: Digital twins create virtual models of physical assets, such as oil rigs and refineries, enabling companies to simulate and optimize operations in real-time. This reduces the need for physical inspections and helps predict potential equipment failures, thereby increasing operational efficiency.

- **Cloud Computing for Data Processing**: The use of cloud-based platforms enables companies to analyze large datasets from multiple sources and collaborate across teams globally. Cloud computing improves data accessibility and scalability, allowing companies to respond faster to changing market conditions.

- **Chevron**: Chevron has embraced cloud computing to enhance its data analysis capabilities and support decision-making across its operations. The company uses cloud platforms to manage real-time data from its oil fields and refineries, improving its ability to optimize production and reduce downtime.

Digital Transformation and Environmental Sustainability

Digital transformation also plays a role in improving the fossil fuel industry's environmental sustainability. By reducing waste, optimizing energy use, and enabling cleaner production processes, digital technologies can help companies lower their carbon footprints.

- **Emissions Monitoring**: Sensors and data analytics are being used to monitor greenhouse gas emissions in real-time, allowing companies to detect leaks, reduce flaring, and minimize emissions. This helps companies comply with increasingly strict environmental regulations and reduce their overall impact on climate change.
- **Reducing Energy Use**: Automation and AI are being used to optimize energy consumption across refineries and production facilities. By reducing energy use and integrating renewable energy into operations, companies can lower operating costs and improve sustainability.
- **Shell**: Shell's use of digital technologies to monitor methane emissions in its operations is helping the company reduce its carbon footprint. The company employs satellite imagery, drones, and real-time monitoring systems to detect and repair methane leaks, significantly reducing greenhouse gas emissions.

Challenges in Implementing Digital Transformation

While digital transformation presents significant opportunities for fossil fuel companies, there are also challenges:

- **High Initial Costs**: The adoption of digital technologies requires significant upfront investments in infrastructure, training, and cybersecurity. Smaller companies may face difficulties in keeping pace with larger industry players in digital innovation.

- **Cybersecurity Risks**: The increased connectivity of IIoT devices and reliance on cloud computing also raises concerns about cybersecurity. Oil and gas infrastructure is a critical component of national economies, and any cyberattacks could have devastating consequences.
- **Workforce Transition**: The shift towards more automated and digitally enabled operations requires new skills among the workforce. Companies must invest in training programs and re-skilling initiatives to ensure their employees can adapt to the new digital landscape.

Conclusion

Digital transformation is helping fossil fuel companies enhance operational efficiency, reduce costs, and minimize environmental impacts in a rapidly changing energy landscape. By adopting technologies such as AI, IIoT, big data analytics, and cloud computing, companies like ExxonMobil, Chevron, BP, and Shell are optimizing production, improving asset management, and enhancing safety while moving toward more sustainable operations. While challenges remain, such as high implementation costs and cybersecurity concerns, the benefits of digital transformation are critical for the industry's ability to adapt to the ongoing energy transition and maintain profitability in the face of declining fossil fuel demand.

5. Corporate Social Responsibility (CSR) and Rebranding

In response to growing environmental concerns, stricter regulations, and shifting consumer expectations, fossil fuel companies are increasingly focusing on **Corporate Social Responsibility (CSR)** and **rebranding** efforts to enhance their reputations and align with the global push for sustainability. Through CSR initiatives and rebranding strategies, these companies are aiming to demonstrate a commitment to environmental stewardship, social well-being, and transparent governance. This approach is also part of a broader effort to maintain their social license to operate and appeal to environmentally conscious investors, governments, and consumers.

Corporate Social Responsibility (CSR) in the Fossil Fuel Industry

CSR in the fossil fuel sector encompasses a wide range of activities designed to address social, environmental, and economic challenges. These companies are increasingly being held accountable for their impact on the environment, climate change, and local communities, prompting them to adopt comprehensive CSR strategies that focus on sustainability, community development, and ethical governance.

Key Areas of CSR Focus

1. **Environmental Stewardship**
    - **Reducing Carbon Emissions**: One of the main pillars of CSR for fossil fuel companies is reducing their carbon emissions and overall environmental impact. Many companies are investing in technologies to lower emissions, such as carbon capture and storage (CCS), renewable energy projects, and energy efficiency improvements in their operations.
    - **Protecting Ecosystems**: Fossil fuel companies are investing in efforts to minimize the impact of oil spills, habitat destruction, and biodiversity loss. They are engaging in reforestation projects, protecting marine ecosystems, and supporting initiatives to restore damaged environments.

- **BP**: As part of its CSR initiatives, BP has committed to reducing its net operational emissions to zero by 2050. The company has also pledged to increase its investments in low-carbon technologies and renewable energy as it transitions to a more sustainable business model.

2. **Social Responsibility and Community Development**

   - **Supporting Local Communities**: Many fossil fuel companies operate in regions where they have a significant impact on local communities. CSR programs often focus on supporting these communities through investments in education, healthcare, and infrastructure development.
   - **Indigenous Rights**: In regions where fossil fuel operations intersect with Indigenous lands, companies are working to engage with Indigenous communities, protect their rights, and ensure that they benefit from local development projects.
   - **Chevron**: Chevron's CSR efforts include investments in community health, education, and economic development in the regions where it operates. In 2020, Chevron launched initiatives to support local businesses and community resilience in response to the COVID-19 pandemic, demonstrating its commitment to social welfare.

3. **Ethical Governance and Transparency**

   - **Sustainability Reporting**: Fossil fuel companies are increasingly adopting sustainability reporting frameworks such as the Global Reporting Initiative (GRI) and the Task Force on Climate-Related

Financial Disclosures (TCFD). These reports help companies provide transparent information about their environmental and social performance.

- **Governance and Accountability**: CSR strategies often include initiatives to improve corporate governance, ensure ethical behavior, and increase accountability. This includes anti-corruption efforts, enhancing board diversity, and implementing policies that promote responsible business practices.
- **Shell**: Shell publishes an annual Sustainability Report detailing its efforts to reduce its environmental impact and contribute to global climate goals. Shell has also committed to transparency regarding its lobbying activities, ensuring that its policy positions align with its publicly stated climate goals.

Greenwashing Concerns

Despite the CSR initiatives undertaken by fossil fuel companies, there are concerns about **greenwashing**—the practice of overstating or misleading the public about a company's environmental efforts. Some critics argue that fossil fuel companies are using CSR and rebranding to deflect attention from their continued reliance on oil and gas production.

To address these concerns, companies are increasingly incorporating third-party verification of their sustainability claims and ensuring that their CSR efforts align with global standards such as the United Nations Sustainable Development Goals (SDGs).

Rebranding Efforts in the Fossil Fuel Industry

As the global energy landscape shifts toward renewables, fossil fuel companies are rebranding themselves as energy companies, reflecting their evolving business models and long-term strategies to move away from a fossil fuel-centric focus

Key Rebranding Strategies

1. **Repositioning as "Energy" Companies** Many fossil fuel companies are rebranding to reflect their expanded focus on renewable energy and sustainable technologies. By rebranding as "energy" companies rather than "oil" or "gas" companies, they aim to signal their commitment to the energy transition and decarbonization.
   - **BP's Rebranding as "Beyond Petroleum"**: BP was one of the first fossil fuel companies to rebrand in the early 2000s, adopting the tagline "Beyond Petroleum" to reflect its commitment to moving toward a sustainable energy future. BP has since shifted much of its focus toward renewables, including wind and solar energy, biofuels, and electric vehicle (EV) charging infrastructure.
   - **TotalEnergies**: In 2021, Total rebranded itself as "TotalEnergies" to emphasize its transition from an oil and gas company to a broader energy company. The new brand reflects the company's growing investments in renewable energy, including wind, solar, and hydrogen, and its ambition to become a leader in the energy transition.
2. **Emphasizing Sustainability in Branding** Fossil fuel companies are incorporating sustainability themes into their branding and marketing, focusing on their role in helping

achieve a cleaner, more sustainable energy future. This includes highlighting their investments in renewable energy, carbon offset projects, and emissions reduction technologies.

- **Shell**: Shell has focused on rebranding itself as a leader in the energy transition, launching campaigns that highlight its investments in renewable energy, electric vehicle charging, and low-carbon technologies. The company's marketing efforts emphasize its ambition to become a net-zero emissions energy business by 2050.

3. **Strategic Acquisitions and Partnerships** As part of their rebranding strategies, many fossil fuel companies are making acquisitions and forming partnerships with renewable energy companies to expand their portfolios and demonstrate their commitment to sustainability.

    - **Chevron**: Chevron has invested in several renewable energy startups and technologies as part of its efforts to diversify its business model. In 2021, Chevron acquired a stake in Zap Energy, a company developing breakthrough fusion energy technologies, signaling its intent to explore clean energy innovations.

4. **Engaging with Stakeholders** Fossil fuel companies are increasingly engaging with stakeholders, including environmental groups, investors, and governments, to develop more credible and effective rebranding strategies. By aligning their branding efforts with stakeholder expectations, companies hope to build trust and enhance their reputations in an evolving energy market.

    - **ExxonMobil**: In 2021, after facing pressure from activist investors, ExxonMobil announced plans to expand its investments in low-carbon technologies and increase transparency regarding its climate strategies. This shift reflects the company's efforts to rebrand itself as more responsive to stakeholder concerns about climate change and sustainability.

Challenges and Criticisms of Rebranding

While rebranding efforts signal a shift toward sustainability, fossil fuel companies face several challenges:

- **Credibility and Authenticity**: Skeptics question whether rebranding efforts are genuine or simply a way to maintain profitability while continuing to produce fossil fuels. Critics argue that real change requires companies to reduce oil and gas production significantly, not just invest in renewable energy.
- **Balancing Profitability and Sustainability**: Fossil fuel companies must balance their desire to reduce carbon emissions and promote sustainability with their need to maintain profitability, particularly given that their core business model still relies on oil and gas production. This tension often leads to criticism that rebranding efforts are more focused on image than substantive change.
- **Investor and Public Expectations**: Rebranding alone will not satisfy investors and the public if fossil fuel companies fail to deliver concrete progress on their sustainability goals. Increasingly, investors are calling for companies to set clear emissions reduction targets, align their business strategies with the Paris Agreement, and improve their ESG (Environmental, Social, Governance) performance.

Conclusion

Corporate social responsibility (CSR) and rebranding have become essential strategies for fossil fuel companies seeking to navigate the challenges of the global energy transition. By investing in environmental stewardship, supporting local communities, and enhancing corporate governance, companies are attempting to demonstrate their commitment to sustainability and ethical business practices. Rebranding efforts, including repositioning as energy companies and emphasizing sustainability, are part of a broader effort to align with global climate goals and appeal to a new generation of consumers and investors. However, companies face challenges in proving the authenticity of these initiatives and must deliver tangible results to avoid accusations of greenwashing and maintain credibility in the eyes of stakeholders.

Conclusion

The fossil fuel industry is undergoing significant changes as it adapts to the realities of global warming, shifting regulatory landscapes, and the global transition toward cleaner energy. In response to declining revenues and increasing environmental scrutiny, companies within the sector are adopting multifaceted strategies that include diversification into renewable energy, investing in carbon capture and storage (CCS), entering new markets like hydrogen and biofuels, embracing digital transformation, and enhancing corporate social responsibility (CSR) and rebranding efforts.

These companies are moving toward sustainability by investing in renewable technologies, aiming to offset their carbon footprint while ensuring long-term profitability. Carbon capture initiatives offer the industry a way to mitigate emissions while continuing oil and gas production, and the exploration of new energy sources like hydrogen and biofuels positions them as key players in the emerging low-carbon economy.

Digital transformation is playing a crucial role in improving operational efficiency, reducing costs, and enabling companies to optimize production while lowering environmental impacts. By integrating advanced technologies such as AI, IIoT, and big data analytics, fossil fuel companies are enhancing safety, productivity, and sustainability.

Simultaneously, CSR and rebranding efforts are helping companies align with global sustainability goals, build trust with stakeholders, and remain relevant in a changing market. However, these initiatives are met with challenges, including accusations of greenwashing, balancing profitability with environmental responsibility, and maintaining credibility amid shifting public expectations.

While these strategies demonstrate a willingness to evolve, the industry still faces significant challenges. Fossil fuel companies must deliver concrete results in reducing emissions and transitioning to cleaner energy to maintain their social license to operate. The success of these efforts will depend on how effectively they can integrate sustainability into their core business models while meeting the expectations of consumers, governments, and investors in the fight against climate change.

In the long term, the industry's ability to navigate this transformation will determine its role in a sustainable future and its capacity to remain profitable in a world that is rapidly moving away from fossil fuels.

Chapter Six
How will it Happen

Lessons Learned from Personal Computers and Cell phones.

One of the problems with long range forecasting is that trends will emerge over 5 or 10 years. that not even in the early stages today, will become major change factors. This problem especially affects major established companies, since they use information about the past to make projections into the future. Sometimes these factors don't involve anything directly with the industry any question.

The COVID-19 pandemic is a good example. In 2019 COVID-19 emerged and for several months it was difficult to predict whether the disease would be contained before it caused significant deaths. From the perspective of research and development there was no way to develop a vaccine for this illness until it emerged. Fortunately, due to herculean efforts a vaccine was developed in just about a year. In the meantime, there was a huge impact upon all the economies of the world and major economic segments within those economies. The hospitality and transportation sectors were significantly affected because it was determined that the disease could be easily transmitted through close personal contact.

The COVID-19 epidemic had some long-lasting impacts on the economy. For example, after being home for several months people realized they could work from home enhanced with new technology. Before Covid commuting to and from work was considered a necessary evil and people had to devote time and expense to commuting. Furthermore, low wage people in industries such as the hospitality changed their perspective on the real benefits of working for a minimum wage.

An examination of two of the most important technological developments which had an impact on people's personal and business lives, are personal computers and cell phones. It is interesting to note that while these trends evolved in established industries the major players were slow to recognize the long-range impact of these new technologies.

Personal computers were first developed by hobbyists and then entrepreneurs expanded the application of these devices to the workplace. Personal computers opened a whole new marketplace for individuals and caused significant change in business. Before personal computers were available. managers had to interact with people in the data processing department who controlled access to and developed applications for centralized data processing. This process was cumbersome. Managers had to communicate to data processing developers their needs and then wait for the applications to be developed often at significant expense.

When the personal computer was first introduced the typical hardware installation cost about $3,000. Managers often had the authority to spend this amount without getting further approval from managers up the line. Once a personal computer was installed reports could be developed using new software packages, which were standardized and thus low in cost. Spreadsheet and word processing programs where the two applications most widely implemented on personal computers because they involved activities that were a major part of business managers activities.

Ironically, IBM noticed these developments and decided to set up a separate business entity to produce personal computers in an effort to capture whatever business might evolve from this new emerging trend. The fact that IBM, the leading company in computing at the time, entered the market was considered an endorsement of this new technology and sales took off exponentially.

The most significant product developed in the 20th century is the cell phone. When cell phone technology was developed in the 80s, it was anticipated that possibly, over the long term there would be a million users. At the time, cell phone usage was expensive because the infrastructure had not yet reached economies of scale. People making projections for the industry assumed that it would be a small market because they were expensive and did not provide significant utility.

Businesspeople who needed to be in touch with their customers and their office while they were on the road saw the value of cell phones even though they were expensive. As with any technology the cost of devices and the services that they used dropped significantly due to economies of scale. This in turn opened the market to the personal use of cell phones.

There is also a significant fact regarding cell phone infrastructure that enabled cell phones to be a worldwide phenomenon not just in developed countries but the entire world. Before the development of the cell phone, there were still a significant part of the world's population that did not have access to communications technology.

If a company was going to implement communication services in a market, it's much more efficient to use cell phone technology. Traditional wireline telephone service requires the installation of poles wires and other facilities in the field. This cause can only be defrayed by the number of users who are near these new facilities. On the other hand, a cell phone company can establish services in a new market by simply installing one tower which will allow all users in the market to access the service regardless of their location. This advantage was so significant that many markets in the developing world which did not have wireline telephone service leapfrogged this service and went straight from nothing to cell phone service.

History may repeat itself in the energy markets for developing countries. Renewable energy can be implemented on a much smaller scale than traditional electricity generated by fossil fuels. In the United States a typical homeowner can install solar panels on the roof of his house and generate electricity for his own use and feed the extra into the grid. Similar investments could be made by individuals in developing countries to provide electricity to join the lifestyle of people in developed countries. When the cost of energy generated by renewable energy comes in parity with the cost of energy generated with fossil fuels developing countries will choose to further expand their renewable energy facilities rather than implement fossil fuel power plants. Once again, the developing world can use a new technology to leapfrog old technology and implement it without having to reach a certain critical mass for much larger electric utilities powered by fossil fuels.

A common criticism made by developing countries is they don't see why they should be asked to restrain their use of fossil fuels when the developed world has already used it and contributed significant CO2 and methane to the atmosphere. Once the cost of renewable energy comes on a par with or is less expensive than traditional fossil fuel energy this argument will no longer be valid.

Furthermore, the demand by developing countries for solar panels, wind turbines and micro-hydroelectric We'll expand the overall demand for these facilities which in turn will lower their costs even more.

I present these examples because the experience with these two changes in technology can provide some insights into how renewable energy will replace fossil fuel energy on a global basis.

Other factors

Unlike personal computer and cell phone technology there is are additional drivers regarding the conversion from fossil fuels to renewable energy. As we all know fossil fuels are the major contribution to carbon dioxide and methane in the atmosphere and these fuels must be eliminated from the economy globally before we experience an existential crisis, so some of the conversion will be mandated further pushing the transition. In addition we do have some experience with renewable energy even though it is still a relatively small component of the global energy market.

Energy is a core component in our economy. Thus, changes in energy markets will impact other segments of the economy. If you want to project the overall impact of the conversion from fossil fuels to renewable energy one must examine both primary and secondary impacts of the transition.

Secondary Impacts

Over the last few years renewable energy Has been considered to be more expensive than fossil fuel energy with the exception of hydroelectric power which has been and still is the cheapest way to produce electricity. Unfortunately dams which are required for hydroelectric power generation have negative environmental impacts in terms of fish migration and land use. While China has often been cited as a major contributor to CO2 emissions because of their widespread application of coal-fired power plants they have been a major implementer of hydroelectric technology. This is probably because the economy is not subjected to the regulations and controls that exist in the United States and Western Europe. As an aside it is interesting to note that Canada still generates most of its electricity via hydroelectric facilities.

Today many consumers are willing to pay a premium for renewable energy as their contribution to the effort to stop global warming. People are so willing to pay more for electric vehicles as their contribution to the same effort. However, we are currently at or very close to the tipping point in the energy market. In any market that is not subject to controls either by monopoly or regulation prices will eventually be set by consumers in the marketplace. When all else is considered price is still the major motivator for consumers. Ironically one of the markets where prices are the major motivator is the gasoline industry. People will drive out of their way or stop when they are passing by a station that allows them to get gasoline for $0.10 or less than a competitive station. Thus, in the long run renewable energy will prevail over fossil fuel energy because it will be cheaper to use.

Gasoline and any other source of energy is a basic commodity. Most people do not make a distinction between one brand or another although many petroleum companies have marketing programs that try to convince people that their product is cleaner or in some way better for your car then their competitors product.

While many consumers may not be aware of it operating an electric vehicle is significantly cheaper than operating a comparable gasoline powered vehicle. In most markets electricity required per mile is about $0.05 per mile as compared to $0.10 to $0.15 per mile for a gasoline powered vehicle. For a consumer that drives 10,000 miles a year this savings will result in an annual saving of somewhere between $500 and $1000.

You may wonder how the operating cost of an electrical vehicle could be so much less than a gas powered one. This is due to two factors 1st The heat required to produce the electric energy that drives the car is much less than the heat required to propel a gasoline powered vehicle. A gasoline engine is not very efficient, it only converts about 20% of the heat in the gasoline fuel to the energy to drive the vehicle. Diesel motors are more efficient which are in the range 40% to 50% regarding converting heat to driving energy. With both the gasoline and diesel engine most of the heat from gasoline fuel is lost. That is why cars have cooling systems which take away the excess heat that could not be converted to driving force.

The second factor is the way electric vehicles operate. When the vehicle is moving forward or accelerating the energy stored in the batteries is used to create the forward motion. When an EV is decelerating or stopping the motor that was driving the vehicle is converted into a generator and places that energy back into the battery of the vehicle. This process slows the vehicle and thus requires less breaking than a gas powered vehicle.

Repair costs for electric vehicles are also significantly lower. Here is an analysis.

As the automotive industry transitions toward electric vehicles (EVs), consumers are increasingly interested in understanding the cost implications of owning an EV compared to a traditional gas-powered vehicle. One of the key factors influencing total ownership cost is **annual repair and maintenance expenses**.

1. Components and Complexity

Gas-powered vehicles have internal combustion engines (ICEs) with numerous moving parts, including pistons, fuel pumps, exhaust systems, transmissions, and cooling systems. The complexity of these components requires more frequent and extensive maintenance, such as oil changes, spark plug replacements, and emission system repairs.

In contrast, **EVs** have far fewer moving parts. Their main components include an electric motor, battery pack, and inverter, which are less prone to wear and tear than ICE parts. EVs also lack parts like oil filters, exhaust systems, and catalytic converters, all of which require regular servicing in gas-powered vehicles.

2. Typical Annual Repair Costs

- **Gas-powered cars** typically incur annual repair costs ranging from **$800 to $1,200** depending on the vehicle model, age, and driving conditions. These costs cover engine repairs, transmission maintenance, exhaust systems, oil changes, and other services.
- **Electric vehicles** generally have lower annual repair costs, averaging around **$300 to $600**. This is largely because EVs require fewer regular maintenance tasks, such as oil changes or exhaust system checks, and have a simpler powertrain design. However, the major cost factor for EVs is the battery, which may require eventual replacement or repair, though this typically occurs after several years.

3. Factors Influencing the Cost Difference

1. **Fewer Mechanical Parts**: EVs have fewer moving parts than gas-powered vehicles, meaning fewer opportunities for breakdowns or repairs. The absence of components like transmission, fuel system, and exhaust significantly reduces repair needs.
2. **No Oil Changes**: Gas-powered vehicles require regular oil changes, typically every 3,000 to 7,000 miles, depending on the vehicle and oil type. EVs do not require oil changes, saving owners approximately **$50 to $100** per change, multiple times per year.
3. **Brake Wear**: EVs use regenerative braking, which reduces wear on the brake pads compared to gas-powered vehicles, where brake pads need more frequent replacement due to mechanical braking systems.

4. **Battery Costs**: The most significant repair-related cost for EVs is the potential replacement or repair of the battery. While this is rare within the first 8 to 10 years due to warranties, when it does occur, it can be expensive, costing several thousand dollars. However, technological advancements are extending battery life, and the cost of replacement is expected to decline over time.

5. **Software and Diagnostics**: EVs rely more on advanced software, which may occasionally require updates or diagnostics. While this can be done remotely or by manufacturers in some cases, it may also lead to specialized service costs.

6. **Specialized Maintenance Services**: Because EVs are newer technology, some repairs or maintenance services must be done by specialized technicians. This could increase labor costs in some regions, though the overall maintenance burden remains lower than that of gas vehicles.

4. Long-Term Maintenance Considerations

- **Gas-powered vehicles** tend to incur increasing repair costs as they age, with components like the transmission, fuel system, and engine wearing out over time. These vehicles also face higher risks of emissions-related repairs as they accumulate miles.

- **Electric vehicles**, in contrast, often have more predictable and lower repair costs over time, with the primary concern being battery longevity. Battery technology improvements and extended warranties (often up to 8 years or 100,000 miles) reduce the risk of significant out-of-pocket costs during the early years of ownership.

In summary, the annual repair costs for EVs tend to be lower than those for gas-powered vehicles due to the simpler mechanical design, fewer moving parts, and reduced need for regular maintenance services. While EV battery repair or replacement can be costly, these expenses are generally rare within the first decade of ownership. For most consumers, the reduced need for engine maintenance, oil changes, and brake repairs makes EVs a more cost-effective option in terms of repairs over the vehicle's lifespan. This trend is likely to continue as battery technology improves and the EV market expands.

Timing of the Demise

How the world transitions from fossil fuel to renewable energy will most likely follow the typical adoption cycle or growth curve for new products. There are some other factors present that are not in a typical new product introduction like the requirement to reduce CO2 emissions by a specific date before we reach a tipping point in global warming. However, in spite of these additional factors one could assume that the transition will still follow a typical adoption cycle for a new product.

The adoption cycles for new products are all fairly similar due to customer driving factors in the cycle. A graph of this change is often referred to as the hockey stick growth curve Because it looks like a hockey stick. On the left-hand side of the chart sales start out at a low level and progress for several months or years at a fairly slow growth rate. Then at a point the growth transitions from the prior years to a very rapid adoption rate where the growth in sales can almost be vertical.

This growth curve can be attributed to several factors of human behavior and market dynamics. When a new product is introduced the first people to purchase the product are referred to as early adopters. These people buy a product simply because it is new and if is it technology intensive product people are enamored with the new technology. Certain people who are early adopters just like being considered people who are hip or in touch with what's going on in the world. People are willing to pay a higher price than the alternative previous product just so they can participate in the new phenomenon. In addition to price there may be some performance issues or a learning curve which makes using the new product less attractive than some existing product. Since there is only a segment of the market that is composed of early adopters, the sales trend in the first year or two are fairly slow.

Once a product starts to mature the original difficulties are ironed out and due to increased volume of production economies of scale start to set in and the price starts to drop in some cases dramatically making the new product cheaper or more efficient then the product it is replacing. This transition can often be quite dramatic, because typical market forces such as lower price and better performance set in for the rest of the marketplace.

On the other end of the spectrum there is a second segment of the market that resists change either because people don't want to go through the learning curve to understand the qualities of the new product or how to use it. However, in the case of replacing fossil fuels that people who resist change may be forced to make a change because regulations require that a product, such as a gasoline powered car they will no longer be sold.

The key take away here is the rapid transition from slow growth to exponential growth transition can take place over a very short period of time. In the case of the fossil fuel industry this dramatic change will be aggravated by the significant assets employed in exploration refining and distribution which will no longer be required. Under normal circumstances businesses depreciate the value of their assets and recognize those as a cost of production over a period of time, usually similar to the expected life of the product or equipment being depreciated. This is what happened with Smith Carona when laser printers replace typewriters. The equipment used to manufacture typewriters had a long life and we're not fully depreciated when the business was no longer viable.

The demise of the fossil fuel industry will be aggravated by the fact that not only do fossil fuel companies employ significant assets in the exploration and refinement of the product they also carry the value of the reserves in the ground for a long period of time until they are extracted and sold in the marketplace.

Another aggravating factor regarding the transition in the fossil fuel industry will be the sheer size of the industry relative to the overall economy. Their resources required to produce the old product cannot be absorbed over a short period of time by other segments in the economy that need similar production capabilities or production employees.

A special factor regarding automobiles

The replacement of gasoline powered vehicles follows a fairly predictable pattern. New cars sold today will remain in operation for about 12 years on average. In the current cycle one gasoline powered car is replaced by another gasoline powered car. Thus, the primary reason for the purchase of new cars to replace older vehicles is the fact that the vehicle wears out. Cars get to the point where repair costs are no longer practical relative to the cost of acquiring a new vehicle, in spite of the fact that used cars are significantly devalued relative to new cars.

Some forecasters are using this 12 year replacement cycle as a reason why the transition from gasoline vehicles to EV's will be buffered or slowed by the desire of vehicle owners to continue to keep one vehicle until it no longer is serviceable. However, it is difficult to calculate how much this replacement cycle will be shortened by the fact that EV's are cheaper to operate than gasoline powered vehicles. It is be reason able to assume that the cycle could be shortened by as much as two years, Or from 12 years to 10 years.

It is even more difficult to predict how the useful life of some products will be reduced by the increased operating efficiency. Heat pumps that operate with electricity can be much more efficient in providing heat for residential heating under some temperature conditions. Many commercial buildings already operate using air conditioning/heat pumps in their HVAC systems.

Renewable energy systems such as solar panels and wind turbines have become more efficient than fossil fuel powered systems. This cost improvement should continue at least for a few more years. When these systems can be operated for a lower cost than fossil fuels systems they will reduce the demand for fossil fuels generating systems.

The price for fossil fuels it's not completely set by the marketplace. The countries that became a part of OPEC the Organization of Petroleum Exporting Countries have been able to control the price of crude oil by limiting production when prices fall below a certain level based on market demand. At some point in the future OPEC countries will no longer be able to control that price of a barrel of crude oil. The recent experience when demand dropped significantly because of the COVID pandemic the price for crude oil dropped significantly because there was nothing that the producing countries could do by limiting production.

When the price of crude oil can no longer be controlled by limiting the output by OPEC countries the world assets deployed in exploration refining and transportation of crude oil we will face the potential of becoming obsolete and drastically devalued

According to Ed Hirs an energy economist at Houston university companies can't break even on oil production when the price of a barrel falls below $45. West Texas intermediate crude oil, the US benchmark, is trading around $71 a barrel recently. In other words, if the price of crude oil should drop by about 37% on a long term basis Companies will no longer be able to operate their production facilities profitably.

Petroleum and gas are used for other purposes other than transportation and heating. Thus, there will be some demand for petroleum and gas for the production of plastics and fertilizer and other non transportation uses even if fossil fuels are completely eliminated from the transportation and heating sector.

Petroleum is used as an input to the production of plastics. This is another product that is under threat due to its environmental consequences on marine life etcetera.

Primary and secondary impacts

In addition to the impact on the major fossil companies there are many other service providers that will also be impacted by the conversion to EVs

Over the last few decades the petroleum distribution market has experienced an uncoupling of the repair business from the gasoline sales. The traditional neighborhood gasoline station where 2 or 4 pumps out front and 3-4 service bays outback has been replaced by super pumpers with 12 to 16 pumps and usually a convenience store. These locations, which gets small margins on gasoline sales, make more profit from the convenience store than from gasoline sales. These locations are adding EV charging stations. While these locations will suffer the loss of gasoline sales over the next couple of decades they most likely will be able to survive on the revenues from convenience store sales and EV charging.

The auto repair business has transitioned from the traditional gasoline station to locations that just do repairs and in some cases concentrate on just one service such as oil changes. These locations will not fare as well with the transition to EV's. If EV's do not require oil changes any location that specializes in this service only will most likely go out of business. Other locations that include tire sales with other services may survive with lower profitability, since tires will still also be required by EV's.

It has been calculated that EV's require about half the expenditure on maintenance as gasoline powered vehicles. Thus, one could assume that the auto repair business will shrink by about one half. It should also be noted that EV can be charged by their owner at home overnight when the vehicle is in the garage. Thus eliminating the need for a visit to a location like a super pumper with a convenience store.

Currently there are 196,643 retail gas stations in the United States. There are approximately 174,500 repair shops that employ 614,433 employees. In 2023 these shops generated $789 billion in revenue. If auto repair business eventually declines to a level 1/2 of today's business, that will result in a revenue loss of about $400 billion without any consideration for inflation.

Fossil fuels must be transported from the location where they are extracted to refineries and then eventually to the end user. As the industry declines there will be less of a need for railroad cars to transfer cool and tanker trucks to transport gasoline and diesel fuel. While it's a relatively small part of the overall market home heating oil must also be transported by trucks to residences.

Depending on where the railroad is located it generates from 15% to 25% of its revenue from the transportation of coal. The revenue of a major crude oil tankers is approximately $5 billion a year.

On the other hand, the Public Utilities that generate electricity and do not sell gas will be positively impacted because they have to provide all the additional electricity for EV's and electrical appliances. At first one could assume that the electric utilities we'll have to make significant investments in infrastructure to accommodate the additional needs for EV's etcetera. However, a fact about the daily production of electricity by power plants may be a moderating impact on this requirement. There is a significant difference between the peak hours electric requirements and electricity required in off hours at night.

Electric utilities already provide time of day pricing for electricity recognizing this daily cycle in demand. A major consideration in the construction of a power generation plant is the need for peak generating capacity. If this peak can reduced it will result in a reduction in the capital requirement to build a new electric generation facility or to upgrade existing facilities.

Since the major part of the increase in demand for electricity will be to charge EV's which can be charged at night during the off hours consumers can get better pricing per kWh and utilities can get better utilization of their power plants and transmission facilities.

What will really happen

As we have illustrated above, the transition from fossil fuels to renewable energy will involve many factors which can be difficult to predict over the period of transition from fossil fuels to renewable energy. It can simply be said that regardless of how rapid the transition is there will be significant impacts as a result of the transition from fossil fuels to renewable energy.

The faster the change the more difficult it will be for companies to adjust to these changes and in some cases there are limited options with regard to participating in the renewable energy business.

Regardless of the speed of the change the change in revenue for various sectors will be very large.Tthus making the problem of accommodating to these changes more difficult.

If a company is in a diversified business and one of its products or services Is replaced by innovation the company can transition people and resources to the new product or service offering. But in the case of the fossil fuel industry where many of companies are selling a single product the transition will be difficult or impossible by transferring resources to other parts of the business.

Oil company actions

Oil companies were the first to discover that burning fossil fuels and the resulting increase in CO2 could lead to global warming. When they realized that this could present an existential threat to their business, they switched to a mode of denying that fossil fuels could lead to global warming. Then as public opinion started to switch to a recognition that fossil fuels were in fact causing global warming several of the oil companies switched their approach to presenting themselves as making efforts to solve this problem. However, these efforts have been minimal in relation to their overall business operations.

It is easy to understand why these companies have taken this approach. They generate significant profits from the sale of fossil fuels which in turn results in significant valuation for the company's shares. Also, the transition to alternative businesses or products will not be easy if at all possible.

In the past other companies have delayed the transition from existing to new products or changing business practices are faced with bankruptcy. At this point the companies either seek to merge with another company that can result in economies of scale or allow the transition of assets to another product. In other cases, companies seek government bailouts since the companies are considered too big to fail.

The economic crisis presented by the failure of fossil fuel companies will be one of the largest crises of all time comparable to the banking crisis that occurred in 2009. As in 2009 even with government assistance some companies will be allowed to fail.

While it may take a decade or more to transition out of fossil fuels to renewable energy some forecasters are anticipating that there will be major changes in the next 5 years. These changes who will be great enough to threaten some of the major companies in the fossil fuel industry. The stock market attempts to anticipate future earnings when valuing the shares of a company. Thus, while the final impacts may not be played out for several years in the future the stock market will try and anticipate these impacts and the valuation of the company's shares. Growth companies trade at price earnings multiples there are many times the value of established companies. These valuations reflect this anticipation. When it goes in the opposite direction consequences can be brought into the present

When a company or an industry is failing the companies that managed to get out in the early stages usually do much better than the ones that stay to the bitter end. Currently investors hold over $4 trillion in fossil fuel industry shares. Solving the global warming problem by transitioning from fossil fuel industries to renewable energy will result in greater negative consequences over the next few years compared to the benefits realized by solving the global warming problem.

Chapter Seven
Planning the Demise

When a service provider must make a wire connection to the customer the only efficient way for the company to provide this service is to have a monopoly on the area it is serving. This is referred to as a regulated monopoly. When AT&T was the major telephone supplier in the United states it was granted a monopoly on providing service in a specific area. . AT&T was allowed to earn an 18% return on its investment provided it maintained 99999 service reliability. 99999 means that only one customer in 100,000 can fail to make a connection. Electric power utilities were also granted franchises in the areas that they served. In many cases today the telephone company, the power company and the cable company share the same telephone pole. Although gasoline sales are a competitive market, governments can have control over certain aspects of the business. For example, when gasoline still contained lead governments set timelines when gasoline had to be lead free. Thus, government already has control of some parts of the fossil fuel industry.

What should we expect from a socially responsible fossil-fuel company in a world threatened by climate change? The answer is simple yet extremely challenging: Such a company and the executives who run it must devote their financial, technical, and political resources toward a just and orderly transition away from fossil fuels. In effect, leaders in the fossil-fuel sector must bring about the end of their industry as we know it.

How should we think about how to proceed? We suggest applying models adopted from the compassionate care of an individual, her loved ones, her caregivers, and everyone involved in the recognition of extreme, if not terminal, care. Society and the fossil-fuel industry face grave challenges. If humanity is to enjoy a stable environment at the end of this century, the fossil-fuel industry cannot continue. Its condition is terminal. Amid such a grim prognosis, three possible forms of treatment are available: triage, euthanasia, and hospice.

We present this assessment to provoke a discussion of a very real dilemma that we face as a society. We are confronted with an existential crisis that requires radical action if we are to respond with adequate scope and scale. The idea of any industry sector bringing about its own demise presents us with some unusual and difficult questions that have relevance for both business management and business education. The magnitude of this specific task compounds the difficulty: There is no more complex and integrated industry sector within which to undertake this exercise than the fossil-fuel sector, and there is no more complex and integrated problem to motivate such an exercise as climate change. If we can address these questions, we can get a better glimpse of the awesome systemic challenge before us.

The Prognosis

The first step in the compassionate treatment of a terminal health condition is helping the patient and loved ones come to terms with the reality that the patient is very sick, is possibly dying, and needs extreme care. Three sets of considerations motivate a terminal prognosis for the fossil-fuel industry.

Acknowledging the full scope of the problem

Climate change is more than an environmental issue. It represents a systemic breakdown with widespread implications for life on this planet. This is not hyperbole—it is the assessment of leading scientists around the world, and this conclusion will forever change the nature of our economies. Human activity is increasing the atmospheric concentration of carbon dioxide, causing a 1°C rise in the average global surface temperature since preindustrial times, and we are struggling to contain continued warming to 2°C by mid-century.

Climate change is one of nine planetary boundaries that scientists have identified and warn that we cross at our own peril. These boundaries represent "thresholds below which humanity can safely operate and beyond which the stability of planetary-scale systems cannot be relied upon." These "key performance indicators" (KPIs) of the planet, as Lancaster University management professor Gail Whiteman calls them, are signaling danger. By exceeding the sustainable boundaries for land system use, pollutants (including plastics), nitrogen and phosphorous waste, and novel chemical releases, we are causing reduced rates of agricultural productivity, degraded marine ecosystems, and, most notably, increased rates of species extinction. This last impact, which scientists call the "sixth mass extinction," could see half of the world's current species disappear by 2100. Much as natural catastrophes extinguished the dinosaurs, viable species today are facing a similar catastrophe through human actions that are altering the planet's ecosystems. In short, through the growth of our population and the economy that supports it, we now influence the biosphere in systemic ways that are unprecedented and that we do not fully understand.

The Bank for International Settlements, an umbrella organization for the world's central banks, warned in 2020 that climate change could generate one of the largest economic dislocations in history.

We must greatly reduce, eliminate, or even recapture greenhouse-gas emissions if global temperature is to be stabilized. Such a radical goal, according to University of Cambridge economist Dimitri Zenghelis, "means that the shape and structure of modern capitalism will have to be changed," [7] as the fossil-fuel sector underpins much of our present-day economy. In addition to this pragmatic diagnosis, we face the moral prognosis that the dire consequences of inaction will be unjustly imposed on the majority of humanity, both now and in the future, by a small minority. As climate activist Duane Elgin asks, "When will humanity express its moral outrage that it is wrong to devastate an entire planet for countless generations to come, just to satisfy the consumer desires of a fraction of humanity for a single lifetime?" [8]

Recognizing the limited scope of economic policy solutions To address climate change, economists recommend carbon pricing to create market signals that will steer corporate strategy and entrepreneurial activity toward less carbon-intensive activities. While important as one tool for dealing with this issue, it will not be enough to catalyze the massive systems change that will reduce carbon emissions to zero in the necessary time scale. It will stimulate only incremental changes, and these will not fundamentally change the system that caused the problem; they will instead continue to make it worse.

To begin, such market adjustments treat the economic system as separate from the planetary system. That is a false premise. The two systems are deeply intertwined, though they change at drastically different paces. The pace of change in the planetary system must dictate the pace of change in the economic system—not vice versa. In 2021, the global average atmospheric concentration of CO2 was 413.2 parts per million (ppm), setting a new record high, jumping 3.3 ppm over 2019 levels and 150 percent above the preindustrial level. That marked the fifth-highest annual increase in the 63 years of the National Oceanic and Atmospheric Administration's records, despite the worldwide economic slowdown from the COVID-19 pandemic. Global mean temperature reached 1.1°C above preindustrial levels, and both emissions and temperature are rising irrespective of the pace of change in our economy. To make matters worse, the rate of CO2 concentration rise is now faster than the 2 ppm per year that scientists had previously predicted. If we don't come to terms with climate change by 2030, damage to the global climate will be irreversible.

But instead of taking immediate, drastic action, we wait for market solutions to develop while the planet is crossing critical environmental thresholds. We will not be able to simply adapt or innovate our way out of this crisis—human life cannot survive at wet bulb temperatures above 35°C, a threshold that some regions around the world have already crossed. In May 2022, for example, India and Pakistan faced a record-breaking heat wave that, according to experts, tested "the limits of human survivability." Even if we stopped increasing CO2 today, the temperature would still rise as previously released emissions continue to overheat the atmosphere. In the end, the scientific and pragmatic reality dictates that we stop burning fossil fuels. This change must happen far more quickly than economic policy solutions alone can realize.

Accepting that substantially reducing greenhouse-gas emissions presents an existential challenge for the industry The economic rationale for hydrocarbon production is based on externalizing costs to human and nonhuman life. As fossil-fuel companies struggle unsuccessfully to be part of the climate solution, they are merely putting forward incremental and limited responses that do not address the core problem.

First, many fossil-fuel companies (and other carbon emitters, such as cement manufacturers) are pinning their hopes on carbon capture and sequestration (CCS) technologies to offset their emissions. But these technologies are not yet market-ready—in fact, most actually emit more CO2 than they capture. In the view of many experts, according to an article in The Climate Herald, it is "not possible for most carbon capture and utilization methods to sufficiently reduce industrial CO2 emissions in time to support the Paris Agreement targets."[16] It would be foolish to bet the future on an unproven technology.

Compassionate Destruction

History has marked the repeated demise of once thriving sectors because of the competitive forces of what Joseph Schumpeter termed "creative destruction," where the market "incessantly revolutionizes the economic structure from within, incessantly destroying the old one, incessantly creating a new one." The typewriter industry disappeared with the rise of personal computers, and the incandescent-lightbulb industry has dimmed as more energy-efficient lighting alternatives, such as compact fluorescent lamps (CFLs) and light-emitting diodes (LEDs), have become more cost competitive.

Creative destruction has also forced individual companies to remake themselves. Finnish multinational Nokia was founded in 1865 as a paper mill and has since expanded into cable, rubber boots, tires, and ultimately telecommunications hardware and software. 3M began in 1902 as the Minnesota Mining and Manufacturing Company, making sandpaper and grinding wheels; today the firm makes a wide variety of products, such as personal protective equipment, window films, dental and orthodontic products, medical products, car-care products, health-care software, and Post-it Notes. But these examples represent adaptation to shifting market conditions, not entire sectors disappearing for non-market-related reasons.

We have also witnessed the end of specific sectors because of government regulation—such as legislation in the United States that banned DDT application in 1972, that gutted the asbestos industry in 1989, and that is poised to end the industry for per- and polyfluoroalkyl substances (PFAS) today. But these sectors were not nearly as intertwined with the global economy and society as fossil fuels.

Today, a vast physical, economic, and political network undergirds the oil, coal, gas, and related chemicals sector. It cannot simply be replaced without massive political, social, and technological disruption. So, instead of "creative destruction," we face the challenge of managing "compassionate destruction," in which we guide all the complex and expansive elements of the fossil-fuel sector through a just and orderly transition to a carbon-free economy.

Choice of Treatment

BlackRock CEO Larry Fink warns, "Divesting from entire sectors—or simply passing carbon-intensive assets from public markets to private markets—will not get the world to net zero." Focusing solely on cutting supply and not reducing demand, he argues, will simply drive up energy prices and encourage more of a backlash against green-energy efforts. But the complexity, centrality, and interconnectedness of fossil fuels in the economy creates a paradox. The demise of the sector must be carefully orchestrated, and that will take time. But the urgency compelled by changes already underway in the natural environment means that the endgame needs to be undertaken quickly.

The patient needs urgent care. To consider such care, we acknowledge that corporations have been endowed with certain rights and responsibilities historically enjoyed by human beings and ask the obvious follow-on question: If a corporation is a person, can a corporation be assisted in death just as a person can be? And, if so, how do we provide compassionate assistance and comfort to the dying patient, as well as to those affected by the passing? To negotiate these questions, we offer three different models for consideration.

Triage is a process where patients entering an emergence room are separated into 3 categories. The first are those who are so seriously injured that no medical efforts will save the patient from eventual death. The second are those who are not seriously injured and may need help recovering in the future but will not immediately die as a result of their injury. Finally, there is the group that is in need of serious medical attention but will more likely survive if that medical attention is provided immediately.

There is one recent example from 2021, when investor Third Point called for Royal Dutch Shell to be split into "multiple stand-alone companies," separating sustainable business lines from legacy fossil-fuel lines. Third Point argued that amputation of the extraction business, designed to maximize the survival of Shell, would force the company to accelerate a shift to lower-carbon businesses while presenting a vision for the corporation's survival after the "operation."[24] In this case, an outside investor prescribed the triage-based approach, but companies in other industries have applied it to themselves. Following the Russian invasion of Ukraine in 2022, bp abandoned its 19.75 percent stake in the Russian fossil-fuel company Rosneft, incurring charges of up to $25 billion.

But triage can also bring about a new kind of entity, becoming truly transformative. In 2022, a billionaire and a Canadian asset-management firm launched an unusual joint bid to take over the Australian energy company AGL Energy and turn it into a renewable-energy company by shutting down its coal power plants earlier than planned

Euthanasia | Our second model, euthanasia, is the act or practice of killing or permitting the death of hopelessly sick or injured individuals (such as persons or domestic animals) in a relatively painless way for reasons of mercy."

Maynard Keynes once called for "the euthanasia of the rentier" class, those who extract profits or rents but do not create wealth in the aggregate economy and who, in the words of Joseph Stiglitz, "destroy wealth as a byproduct of their taking it away from others." At present, fossil-fuel companies produce petroleum that is burned to support our economy but create greenhouse-gas emissions that are destroying wealth for others, through the facilitated increase in droughts, wildfires, food insecurity, water scarcity, coastal flooding, disease proliferation, and the social unrest that may result. A future in which we address climate change may require that the entire sector be euthanized.

Deciding on corporate euthanasia compassionately demands a deliberative process. For example, in 1964, the US Surgeon General recommended that drastic controls on cigarette smoking be established to protect public health. Tobacco companies such as R.J. Reynolds and Brown & Williamson stood to lose billions of dollars in revenues if cigarettes were linked to cancer, and mounted a multipronged campaign to create doubt and confusion in the science of cigarette-caused cancer. as a result, it took four decades for cigarettes to be controlled by government regulation, and countless people were made sick or died as a result. But finally, in 1998, the four largest US tobacco companies entered into the Tobacco Master Settlement Agreement (MSA), which required the companies to make annual payments to the 46 participating states in compensation for medical costs of caring for people with smoking-related illnesses. The MSA also dissolved several tobacco trade groups (such as the Tobacco Institute) and prohibited most forms of tobacco advertising.

An important step in euthanasia is coming to terms with the extreme decision facing the patient, the doctor, and those affected by the outcome. Many actors in the fossil-fuel industry have denied climate science and funded campaigns of misinformation and misdirection, like the tobacco industry did, to prevent action addressing climate change.[33] Today, the fossil-fuel sector continues to shift responsibility away from corporations and uses the rhetoric of consumer demand to individualize responsibility. It is not ready to face the prognosis that confronted the tobacco industry; rather, it continues to focus on what it does best: finding, extracting, refining, and marketing fossil fuels.

In fact, fossil-fuel companies have taken little concrete climate action and continue to exploit the markets for fossil fuels, according to a recent study of their annual reports, earnings, and expenditures. For example, in the face of declining markets for fossil fuels precipitated by, among other things, the electrification of the automobile fleet, fossil-fuel companies have sought new markets. Most notably, attention is shifting to chemical production and, more specifically, plastics. The World Economic Forum predicts a doubling of plastics production by 2035 and a quadrupling by 2050, and projects that by 2050 the world's oceans will contain more plastic than fish (by weight).

The patient is in denial about its terminal condition and is engaged in bargaining. For example, the industry's ongoing hope that carbon capture and sequestration will save it resembles a terminally ill patient holding out for a miracle cure. The fossil-fuel sector is showing limited signs that it can restrain itself from finding, extracting, refining, and marketing fossil fuels. Yet, like the tobacco industry in the past, fossil-fuel companies are now facing lawsuits from state's attorneys general for misleading the public about climate change and the dangers of using fossil fuels.

Hospice Our third model, hospice, can be triggered if the patient comes to accept his or her terminal condition. The US National Institute on Aging explains hospice as a treatment regimen that "provides comprehensive comfort care as well as support for the family, but … attempts to cure the person's illness are stopped. Hospice is provided for a person with a terminal illness whose doctor believes he or she has six months or less to live if the illness runs its natural course."

Just as doctors are trained to preserve the patient, business leaders are trained to preserve the business. While bankruptcy and liquidation are situations that many of them face, these decisions are not undertaken when individual business financials are sound. Yet, as doctors have become increasingly concerned with the quality of life, not with merely prolonging its duration, business leaders must do the same, determining when there exists no viable path that can balance the needs of the Earth and humanity against those of the corporation. They must plan for death of an organization, a decision that affects many stakeholders in multiple ways and has a comparable emotional journey for those most involved. Employees often tie their identities to their work and deciding to let go and move on can be challenging for them. For customers, investors, suppliers, and others, that critical decision may be equally vexing.

Signs that this treatment regimen is possible are emerging, as some leaders within the fossil-fuel sector are discussing whether their prognosis is terminal. While many continue to remain in one of the first four stages others are moving toward accepting that the science of climate change is real and that their industry is the chief cause of the crisis. For example, the International Energy Agency, a multilateral group whose mandate is to assure global energy security and stability, issued a report in 2021 that called for investment in new oil and natural-gas projects to stop immediately, and for sales of new gasoline- and diesel-powered vehicles to end by 2035, so that the global energy industry can achieve net-zero carbon emissions by 2050.

Critical to this deliberative process is a sense of control and dignity, something hospice seeks to provide by managing physical, social, and emotional complexities. The core of the hospice approach is the belief that each of us has the right to die pain-free and with dignity, and that families will receive the necessary support to do through compassionate care, counseling, and support to surviving family and friends. In the same way, corporate hospice can help those within or associated with a company or sector to come to terms with and plan for the end of what they know and to look toward what is to come.

Whatever form it takes, death is not merely an end but the beginning of a transformation into something else—whether that something else is a spiritual transition of the soul or the physical transition of the body. In a similar way, does the complex network that constitutes the fossil-fuel sector truly die, or does it become something new? Just as in organ donation, some of the sector's economic and human assets may be redeployed toward some new purpose. People working in the industry have incredible financial, analytical, and geophysical expertise that can (and should) be recognized as a potential asset for a sustainable future.

Managing the End

Estimates of how much money is needed for an energy transition away from fossil fuels over the next three decades range from $50 trillion to $150 trillion.[45] This amount represents both historic entrepreneurial opportunities and massive dislocations with collateral issues that must be managed for a just and orderly transition. Models of triage, euthanasia, or hospice challenge the corporate manager in new and unusual ways. A process of compassionate care and treatment requires a leader to understand the complexity of the corporate ecosystem and identify leverage points for innovation and change on at least four levels: the corporation, the economy, the broader society, and ultimately leadership itself. We specifically suggest 10 sets of critical considerations and questions.

Manage Business Strategy

The implications of triage, euthanasia, or hospice for a corporation are acute and require careful deliberation for an orderly transition. Corporate leaders face a series of considerations as they assume responsibility for how this treatment regimen might affect their employees and the communities in which they operate.

1. Bring about the end of the entire sector through corporate collaboration. The closure of the fossil-fuel sector will require the participation of and collaboration among a wide array of actors. Not only public companies like ExxonMobil, bp, Total SA, and Chevron but national oil companies that underpin the economies of countries such as China, Saudi Arabia, Russia, Brazil, India, Iran, and Venezuela will have to participate. If one fossil-fuel company were to merely cease production, another player would take its place, one that could be less scrupulous about environmental, social, safety, and political standards. This level of global cooperation is on a scale we have never encountered before.

One business model for managing collective action is "precompetitive collaboration," where industry leaders work to find consensus on the future direction of the fossil-fuel sector and the economy as a whole.[46] Precompetitive collaboration uses an iterative and collaborative framework that brings together all the relevant actors to coordinate their concerns, priorities, and actions. In this way, attention can move beyond incremental solutions to address the root causes of issues from multiple, diverse vantage points. As such, this process must involve not only the CEOs of the world's fossil-fuel companies but also representatives from governments, trade associations, research centers, environmental activism, local Indigenous groups, and many other parties.

2. *Protect workers and avoid labor flight during transition.* Just as compassionate care of a dying patient requires comforting family members and friends, a just and orderly transition means not leaving people behind.[47] When a company announces a plan to end its fossil-fuel activities, will employees who have opportunities elsewhere flee the company, leaving it short of talent to execute its plans? How will the loss of jobs be managed? Some skills can be readily transferred (e.g., accountants and salespeople), while others are largely industry specific (e.g., oil-field roustabouts). Estimates of the number of people employed in the fossil-fuel sector vary widely, ranging from 1 million to 2.6 million. The US Bureau of Labor Statistics estimates that 565,000 people work in the mining, quarrying, and oil and gas extraction sector, and 133,300 people work in the oil and gas extraction subsector. If fossil-fuel consumption were largely eliminated over a 20-year period (an extreme scenario), some economists calculate an average of 53,600 jobs lost annually.

As fossil-fuel industries decline, the transition must be managed with dignity, offering displaced workers job retraining, education, and pensions to thank them for helping to bring about a modern world. This effort also might mean identifying parallel opportunities in industries that need similar skill sets (e.g., geothermal drilling, carbon-capture tracking, new lobbying priorities). Just as when a patient is dying, we need to make sure their dependents are cared for. Such care requires a clear vision and plan for transition that can foster inclusion and catalyze long-term reform that invigorates talented employees with new challenges to tackle.

AT&T went through several major transitions as a result of reorganization or technology change. The company once employed about a million people as operators. When digital switches were deployed almost all these people were no longer required. The company offered employees several options based upon their status with the company employees near retirement were offered early retirement other employees were offered the opportunity to transfer to other parts of the company and finally some were offered substantial buyouts which allowed them the resources necessary to maintain their lifestyle while they look for employment elsewhere.

As a result of divestiture AT&T was broken up into several major different companies. It was the long-distance company a Regional Bell Operating Companies the research company Bell Labs and the manufacturing operations that made switches telephones and other equipment required for their communications business.

When these companies became separate entities the former Bell system allowed people to transfer from one company to another as if they were just making a transfer within the old company. In other words, they maintain their seniority and other benefits as if they were still being employed by the same company.

3.Overcome political and social resistance to change

A decline and end of the fossil-fuel sector will precipitate political, economic, and social blowback. Those who stand to lose out in the transition will fight hard to protect what they have. In several states, the conservative lobbying group American Legislative Exchange Council (ALEC) is recommending laws to blacklist firms that boycott the fossil-fuel industry as a way to protect fossil-fuel companies from share sell-offs and other measures intended to address the climate crisis.

In a January 2022 public letter to Texas Comptroller Glenn Hegar, Lieutenant Governor Dan Patrick called out BlackRock's Fink for "capriciously discriminating against the oil and gas industry" and declared, "If Wall Street turns their back on Texas and our thriving oil and gas industry, then Texas will not do business with Wall Street." [54] The fossil-fuel industry is economically and culturally central to states such as Texas, and the basis of national prosperity and geopolitical power for nations such as Saudi Arabia, Venezuela, and Russia. Corporate leadership will need to identify stakeholders and involve them in the transition and its consequences. Just as end-of-life planning involves the preparation of a will, a just and orderly transition includes a plan to help those left behind.

Manage Broader Economic Impacts

The effects of corporate triage, euthanasia, or hospice are not isolated to the companies undergoing these processes themselves. The fossil-fuel industry has impacts on the broader economy that must be managed, just as the impacts of a dying person on family members, friends, and colleagues must be negotiated.

4. *Account for the full scope of the financial impact of the transition.* The emergent, clean-energy sector is growing rapidly. Some estimates report an employment base of nearly 3.3 million Americans, outnumbering fossil-fuel workers by upwards of 3 to 1. This growth is driven in large part by technological innovation and policy choices. The average installed cost of wind power dropped from 7 cents per kWh in 2009 to less than 2 cents in 2019. Solar photovoltaic power saw a 99 percent decrease in price between 1980 and 2012

The top 10 fossil-fuel companies in the world enjoy a market capitalization of $4.1 trillion. Sixty of the world's largest commercial and investment banks collectively invested $3.8 trillion in fossil fuels from 2016 to 2020 In the first nine months of 2021, the 24 largest oil and gas companies netted $174 billion in profits, and 11 of them paid out $36.5 billion collectively to shareholders. How will these investments be maintained and transitioned? If a company announces a plan to end its fossil-fuel activities, will investors flee the company, leaving it short of capital to execute its plans? Similarly, will those investors who stay with the company watch their capital diminish? Finally, should fossil-fuel companies and their investors be compensated for fossil fuels left in the ground—fuel that was factored into the valuation of these companies and drew investors in the first place?

5. *Control the fate of products both used and unused.* There are 1.65 trillion barrels of proven oil reserves in the world, which amount to 46.6 times the world's annual consumption levels and will last at least another 50 years[5] The International Energy Agency predicts a peak in demand between 2020 and 2040; the Organization of the Petroleum Exporting Countries (OPEC) predicts increasing demand, followed by a plateau after 2035. If that oil is burned, scientific modeling predicts that we will not be able to keep planetary temperatures at levels that are safe for human life. But how do we manage what will become a "stranded asset," both avoiding a black market and allowing for an equitable solution? What will prevent defectors from extracting that valuable oil?

6. *Protect indirect workers in related industries.* For each fossil-fuel worker directly affected by the end of the fossil-fuel sector, there are additional jobs that depend on the sector. In India, every coal miner on a monthly salary generates up to 10 additional local jobs through their consumption. If the coal miner's job is lost, these other local jobs also disappear. In the United States, the fossil-fuel industry provides nearly 7.2 million indirect jobs. For example, the oil and natural-gas industry purchases capital goods from a variety of US suppliers; these amount to $177 billion in new equipment and structures. Even companies that proclaim to reject fossil fuels (e.g., clothing suppliers) depend on petrochemicals derived from oil and natural gas. These kinds of impacts can be regional in their scope, and efforts to protect regional economies should be part of the energy transition.

Manage Societal and Policy Issues

Decisions about corporate triage, euthanasia, and hospice are made more difficult not only by these considerations but by other complex societal impacts. Corporate leaders must consider the process and distribution of these impacts to weigh the equity of who will bear the costs.

7. *Maintain justice and equity for all communities.* Millions of jobs in the fossil-fuel industry could be displaced by 2050. But these displacements will not fall evenly and will affect some communities more than others. In Wyoming, for example, nearly 8,400 people are employed in coal and nearly 68,000 are employed in natural gas and oil; these industries in total provide about 16.6 percent of jobs in the state. In addition, more than half of state and local tax revenues come from the fossil-fuel sector. Other states that are heavily dependent on the industry include Oklahoma, North Dakota, Texas, Louisiana, Alaska, New Mexico, and West Virginia. The economies in these states could be devastated if the industry were to decline and no provisions were made to offset the economic impact, in much the same way as the departure of manufacturing jobs turned midwestern US economies into the rust belt in the 1980s. Fossil fuels are still an enormously important source of employment across the world, and fossil-fuel jobs often offer higher salaries and better benefits than most jobs.

As the fossil-fuel industry declines or disappears, how will the economies of developing countries be protected? Can they make the infrastructure investments to transition their economies to non-carbon-based fuels and jobs? And can they protect themselves from efforts by fossil-fuel interests to extract rents for lost revenues? In 2021, fossil-fuel companies were suing governments across the world for more than $18 billion after action against climate change threatened their profits. They brought these suits under the Energy

Charter Treaty, and the proceedings are being hosted within the International Centre for Settlement of Investment Disputes, a branch of the World Bank beyond the reach of the countries' domestic legal systems.

8. *Decommission, remediate, and repurpose dedicated infrastructure.* We must also address the enormous legacy infrastructure associated with the fossil-fuel sector. The United States alone has more than 2.6 million miles of fossil-fuel pipelines, 129 operable petroleum refineries,75 thousands of train cars and tanker trucks, approximately 542,000 underground storage tanks and a comparable number of aboveground storage tanks, and more than 150,000 fueling stations (95 percent of which independent operators own) to fuel 287 million registered cars and 38 million trucks. Globally, there are more than 600 operating refineries[7]and 810 very large crude carriers (one VLCC can transport more than two million barrels of crude oil). How will these assets be redeployed or decommissioned? Further, an enormous legacy of hazardous waste looms from coal mining; oil exploration, refining, and transport; and shale-gas development that will require extensive remediation. Who will pay for it?

9. *Leverage the power of government.* The energy transition that is underway requires the involvement and unprecedented cooperation of governments from around the world. They have, and must continue to play, a critical role in determining the rate of innovation to no-carbon technologies through tax policies, subsidies, loan guarantees, procurement, and research-and-development support. At the least, governments must remain committed to carbon-reduction goals, such as those set by the Paris Agreement, to establish clear market signals for companies. The Norwegian oil company Equinor has made it clear that to meet its goal of allocating more than half of its annual gross capital expenditures to renewables or low-carbon solutions by 2030, it needs European and global leaders to stick to their climate commitments. Governments must also reduce, eliminate, or repurpose the $423 billion in subsidies for the fossil-fuel industry annually; help economically at-risk fossil-fuel workers through retraining; support local businesses; and invest in associated infrastructure. Finally, the power of government must be maintained in the face of pressure from incumbent fossil-fuel companies and their lobbying power as they spend nearly $200 million per year to delay, control, or block policies to tackle climate change.

Manage the Role of Corporate Leadership

Ultimately, decisions about corporate triage, euthanasia, and hospice require a new form of corporate leadership. The training of business leaders must be revised to cover all facets of the systemic changes such decisions entail, including transformations of the corporation, the economy, and society.

10. *Overhaul business education as if people and the planet really matter.* As these grave forms of treatment—triage, euthanasia, and hospice—and the list of critical, related questions make clear, transitioning away from the fossil-fuel sector is a monumental systemic challenge. It will require strong and thoughtful leadership from all within the fossil-fuel sector, as well as from leaders in business, government, and civil society. And, importantly, it will require a reassessment of how we train those future leaders. These needs must guide the transformation of business education.

Many business schools in the United States, the European Union, and elsewhere have begun to recognize the growing urgency of climate change and are incorporating the issue more centrally into their curricula. They are especially motivated by the scale of the market shift that climate change demands, which could range as high as $26 trillion through 2030 and create 65 million new low-carbon jobs. These schools are also desperate to avoid more than 700,000 premature deaths from air pollution. In response, they are gearing their curricula toward the development of new products, services, and practices and examining ways to transform business models, technology, and innovation.

These efforts, while critical, are missing a crucial component by focusing on only one side of the equation: the financial opportunity or the win-win. Schools tend to pay little, if any, attention to the other side of the equation: the eventual win-lose in some sectors. Given this gap, they are not preparing students to lead a just and orderly transition, which will require tough choices if we are to address the full scope of our climate problems. Business schools teach students how to launch, grow, and maintain companies, but not how to sunset them. Tomorrow's business leaders should be taught to do something that previous generations rarely did: They must start to think critically about the role of business in society, their role as managers in guiding those businesses, and the overall system in which they will practice their craft.

The host of considerations we have offered, and many more, open new avenues of inquiry for teaching important aspects of the role of business in society and how it will operate in the 21st century. The skills to dismantle an industry as complex and integrated as the fossil-fuel sector can help students develop a deeper understanding of the complex network that is the modern multinational corporation. To undertake such a task while the company is still financially viable brings the topic into a new domain, distinct from more straightforward considerations of bankruptcy and liquidation.

Chapter Eight
Conclusion

An alternative scenario

We would like to conclude this book with a scenario that involves a world without fossil fuels. Let's assume that millions of years ago plant life did not die and then become compressed and turned into fossil fuelss

As we described in the beginning of this book fossil fuels drove the industrial revolution. We could assume that the industrial revolution would never have occurred and we'd still be riding on horseback or horse drawn carriages and living in homes that were heated with wood. However, the development of technology and resources is driven by the resources that are available to fill the need at the time. We suggest that the economy would have taken a different path if fossil fuels were not available, but progress may not be as hindered as one might expect.

The first energy harnessed by humans to enhance their efforts was waterpower. Waterpower had been used for centuries before the beginning of the industrial revolution to mill grain, pump water and saw lumber. We all have seen an old mill with the water wheel on the side 15 or 20 feet in diameter which captured the energy of falling water that turned a millstone to grind grain into flour. There are thousands of these mills scattered around the northeast United States and many of them still exist today as tourist attractions or converted to some other use like restaurants. Though less visible to the casual observer there are also mills that use a horizontal wheel that captures the power of a stream flowing under the mill to turn a millstone.

The industrial revolution started with waterpower. The city of Paterson, NJ, which is located on the Passaic River is often referred to by many as the birthplace of the industrial revolution because it harnessed the power of water falling over the Great Falls to produce mechanical energy that was used in the mills on the riverbank. Although the manufacturing in Paterson NJ has moved elsewhere, the river is still being used to produce power. At the base of the falls is a 12 MW hydroelectric facility. While relatively small compared to other power plants it still generates enough electric power for about 5000 homes.

We all know Thomas Edison is known for the invention of the light bulb. He also designed the facilities to generate electricity used by these light bulbs and other electrical appliances. A turbine to generate electricity can be driven by water or steam. If coal was not available to create the steam necessary to turn a turbine waterpower could be used in its place. At one time up to 45% of the electricity generated in the United States came from hydro generating facilities. Before electrical wires were built out into rural areas, manufacturing facilities and homes generated their own electricity via hydropower. If you walk in the wooded area around some of these estates and manufacturing facilities, you can still see the remains of the hydroelectric generating facility.

Hydroelectric power now contributes about 6% of the total energy generated in the United States. However, the Department of Energy has determined in studies that if all the dams located in the US we're retrofitted with generating capabilities power output could be increased by 150%. In other words, the 6% could become 15%.

While hydroelectric power is still the most efficient way to generate electricity it has been in decline because of negative environmental consequences. Some of the dams built just for hydroelectric production have been removed and others are scheduled to be removed. Many of the dams that could be retrofitted to produce hydroelectricity have another primary purpose, either flood control or providing reservoirs that balance the flow of drinking water from the winter months when rain is more frequent to the summer months when the heat requires an increase in water consumption.

Many drinking water systems have facilities referred to as stilling chambers, which are required to dissipate the energy in the water coming from higher altitudes before it is put into the local water supply system. If this energy was not dissipated it would blow out facilities not designed to have such high-water pressure. Much of the energy in these systems is being wasted.

Windmills have been used for many years to pump water. The classic example is the windmills in Holland where mulch of the land is below sea level. In the early days of farming and ranching in the United States windmills were used to pump water. Today the average wind turbine is a massive structure that generates about four megawatts of electricity. These windmills have been developed in recent years to generate renewable energy to replace energy from fossil fuels. If fossil fuels were not available in the past to generate electricity, wind turbine similar to those today would have been developed to meet the need at that time.

About 20% of the electricity generated in the US comes from nuclear facilities. Almost all of these facilities were built between 1970 and the early 1980s. After a period of very rapid growth output has stabilized at the current level of about 20% of total electrical power production. Current nuclear plants employ fission technology to generate energy. Recent breakthroughs in the design of fusion facilities indicates that this technology might be commercially viable sometime in the next 10 to 20 years If not sooner. Currently Microsoft is considering reactivating the nuclear generating facility at Three Mile Island that was not damaged by the meltdown at that facility. The power from this facility will be used at a company facility to power all the computers required to support artificial intelligence

My primary purpose here is not to give you an understanding of these three ways of generating electricity but rather to indicate that the utilization of these potential generating capabilities might have evolved on a much different timeline if fossil fuel energy was not available Thus, I believe that much of the progress we have experienced in increased living standards since the beginning of the industrial revolution would still have happened. We would have just used different sources of the electrical energy that we needed to run our electrical appliances.

When the automobile was first being developed There was a debate whether cars should be powered by electric motors or gasoline engines. When electricity was first developed there was a debate whether the energy should be delivered either through alternating current AC or direct current DC. Thomas Edison was the major backer of AC and Tesler was the major backer of DC. When Elon Musk started is automobile business, he named it Tesler to honor the man who was left behind by the growth of AC.

There are many instances when new technology was developed there were two alternatives to use this technology. This was true with video cassette recorders, microcomputers, and cell phones. The winning technology is chosen because it performs the task at hand more efficiently or with more features.

According to one feminist whose name I cannot recall indicated one of the reasons why in the early days of the automobile it was decided to go with a gasoline powered engine rather than an electric motor powered by batteries was the fact that gasoline powered engines we're dirtier and grimier, which appealed to males who would be the primary decision makers in acquiring an automobile. Women preferred electric vehicles because they were much easier to start and operate. Another reason why gasoline was selected is that it was an available source of power relative to the bulk of the gasoline. Electric batteries were not as efficient, but if gasoline was not available a lot of the improvements that we have seen in the storage capacity of batteries might have taken place earlier if that was the only alternative available to powering automobiles.

One could say trucks would not have been developed to haul goods because diesel fuel was not available. However electric powered locomotives replaced steam locomotives many years ago. Railroads might still be used to haul a lot more of our goods. at least long distances.

It has been my experience that the development of technology or research in general does not follow some preordained timeline. The primary determinant in the progress of technology and knowledge in general is the amount of effort and resources devoted to research or solving a particular problem. At the height of the AIDS epidemic the amount of money spent on research to cure AIDS was multiples of the amount of money being spent on cancer research. Today AIDS is basically under control whereas we still have a long way to go to solve all cancers.

At the beginning of the 1960s President Kennedy set a national objective of going to the moon before the end of the decade. This was accomplished although much of the technology that was required to accomplish this task did not exist at the beginning of this effort.

The purpose of this scenario has been to illustrate that while the fossil fuel industry had a lot to do with the development of the living standards that we enjoy today it would most likely be true that we would have accomplished most of these things without the fossil fuel industry. I will grant that fossil fuels were the most expeditious way of achieving our development objectives, but they were not the only course of action that we had then or we have today.

Fossil fuels must be eliminated

Simply stated, a major portion of the fossil fuel industry must be eliminated in order to allow humans to maintain the lifestyle we have become accustomed to. Ironically, the industry that contributed the most to the development of the life cycle we enjoy today is the fossil fuel industry.

Even if we are able to replace the fossil fuel industry with renewable energy in the next decade, we will still suffer significant economic loss as a result of the global warming which has already contributed to climate change. The extra CO2 and methane put into the atmosphere since the birth of the industrial revolution will continue to have effects for hundreds or thousands of years in the future.

The major focus of the media and the business community has been on the economic impacts global warming will have on society. Little attention has been directed at the cost of eliminating the fossil fuel industry. There are some projections that this cost could be between $50 trillion and $150 trillion. To put this in perspective the entire GDP of the world economy is currently around $100 trillion.

The progression of global warming compared to projections made five years ago indicates that global warming is progressing just about as expected. These projections indicate that we will reach a tipping point or the point at which will be beyond our control. That point is around 2035, or 10 years in the future.

The fossil fuel industry is one of the biggest segments of the global economy and it has failed to recognize the threat it has created to our lifestyle today. Other major segments of the economy such as tobacco industry refused to recognize the negative impact it was having on society until it was forced to make changes in its behavior. When these segments finally face the music, the consequences have been greater than what they could have been if they had recognized the issue sooner and taken appropriate mitigating actions.

While these industries were large, they were not integrated into the overall economy to the extent as the fossil fuel industry. Thus, while the consequences were significant where the companies operated the overall economy was not significantly impacted. This will not be the case with the fossil fuel industry. The consequences of the demise of the fossil fuel industry, if not handled properly could be as great as the consequences of allowing global warming to run its course. To make matters worse the consequences of the demise of the fossil fuel industry could occur in the relatively short term compared to the unfolding of the impacts from global warming which may take as long as 50 years even if conditions are stabilized.

There is an old saying that the worst thing you don't know is the thing you don't know you don't know. In other words, if you have a problem, you can't solve it until you know you have a problem. In the last year the news reads like an apocalyptic novel as our world has witnessed unprecedented heat waves wildfires and flooding around the globe what the New York Times calls this summer of climate disasters nearly 2/3 of Europe suffered a worst dry spell in 500 years the American southwest suffered heat waves unseen in 1200 years and China experienced the most extreme heat wave ever recorded on earth. Britain saw temperatures above 40°C or 104°F. This has led to droughts farmed, water shortages, wildfires, power outages, transportation disruptions and deaths. Reservoirs in Spain have dropped below 30% capacity two of the largest reservoirs in America lake Mead and Lake Powell almost reached Deadpool status many rivers in Europe China and elsewhere are drying up the Danube is flowing at less than half its usual summer volume leaving dozens of cargo ships to lie motionless. Pakistan has experienced unprecedented flooding because of a monsoon on steroids washing away 45% of the country's cropland and impacting an astonishing 33 million people.

And yet in the same time, global taxpayer subsidies to the fossil fuel sector almost doubled to $500 billion, while the sector is recording record profits.

Meanwhile the political debate over what action to take rages on. To secure the votes of major businesses candidate Donald Trump has promised if he is elected to eliminate most environmental legislation and even dismantle some of the government agencies that monitor worldwide weather conditions. Although The United States is already the largest producer of fossil fuels in the world, he has promised to allow additional exploration and drilling for oil.

In this book we have shown how we arrived at the situation we are in today. We have shown that we are faced with the requirement of replacing one form of energy technology with another. With the proper perspective the implementation of renewable energy to replace fossil fuel energy is the magic bullet that some people think we can develop to save all the problems that we currently experience.

In times of crisis people have been known to put aside their differences to do whatever it takes to solve the problem at hand. Probably in the entire course of human history we are now faced with the largest problem ever.

For people to put aside their differences and become unified behind a solution a true unbiased understanding of the situation is essential. This book is an effort to create that understanding and common objective.

www.ingramcontent.com/pod-product-compliance
Lightning Source LLC
LaVergne TN
LVHW100311210926
848480LV00003B/1094
* 9 7 8 1 9 1 7 6 3 6 8 5 8 *